# THE
# REMARKABLE
## PRACTICE

# THE
# REMARKABLE
## PRACTICE

### THE DEFINITIVE GUIDE TO BUILDING A THRIVING CHIROPRACTIC BUSINESS

## DR. STEPHEN FRANSON

LIONCREST
PUBLISHING

THE REMARKABLE PRACTICE
*The Definitive Guide to Building a Thriving Chiropractic Business*

ISBN  978-1-5445-0239-7  *Hardcover*
       978-1-5445-0237-3  *Paperback*
       978-1-5445-0238-0  *Ebook*

*This book is dedicated to my son, Sam, who at this point says that he wants to be a Chiropractor when he grows up. So do I. Regardless of the path that he chooses, I am infinitely proud of him. He has been my greatest teacher—this is my chance to pay him back.*

# CONTENTS

# THE RUBIK'S CUBE OF PRACTICE SUCCESS

If you've picked up this book, it's safe to say that you want to grow your practice. You want to do more, serve more, give more, and make more. You want to make a bigger impact and a better income. I'm guessing that you are an "On-Purpose" Chiropractor who is Mission-Driven. I'll assume that the reason you got into Chiropractic in the first place was to serve others and make the world a healthier and happier place. And I'll bet that you started with a Vision of your practice being a place where people would find a better way to better health.

If you are like me, you know that we are in the business of saving lives—and if business is good, everybody wins. Because of this, you are driven to grow—to build your practice and become even more "successful."

But here's the rub: **you don't want to become "successful"** *at the expense of* **your marriage, your relationship with your kids, your health...your life.**

Sometimes it seems like you're damned if you do and damned if you don't. You probably already feel overworked and out of balance; maybe even overwhelmed. It seems like in order to grow your practice, you're going to have to put in even more time and more energy, and work even harder, faster, longer. Really?

*How would that even be possible?* you think to yourself. And would the tradeoff be worth it, if it meant giving up so much of your life? You may even end up questioning your Vision.

Moreover, how could you continue to talk about the Chiropractic Wellness Lifestyle out of one side of your mouth while killing *yourself* to become "more successful" in the process?

*Isn't that a huge contradiction?* Or is that just how it is? Maybe the only way to grow your practice and achieve the success you're looking for is indeed to sacrifice everything else in your life and trade dollars for hours. Right?

**Wrong.**

## A REMARKABLE PRACTICE AS *PART* OF A REMARKABLE LIFE

When I'm speaking from the stage and say, "You are in the business of saving lives, and when business is good everybody wins" most DCs close their eyes, smile, and nod their heads in agreement. But, I am usually only two or three probing questions away from revealing the truth—and that is that most chiropractors don't own a business at all. They own a job—or more accurately, **they have created a job that owns them**.

So for most doctors, the idea of growing the practice means more time, more energy, more work, more stress, and more imbalance. And here lies the contradiction. You want to build your practice and become more "successful," but you don't really want to grow because you think that it would have serious negative consequences to the quality of your life.

Now, imagine doubling your practice. Pause on that thought for a second. How does that feel, honestly? If your practice volume was to double next week, what would break? Would you actually want to double your practice? How about if I asked your staff—your Team? Would they want to double?

Here's the thing, doubling your practice *doesn't* have to mean taking what you're currently doing and doubling it.

**I'll suggest that there's a better way.** A different way—an approach to practice that creates a dynamic where growth becomes the natural expression of your practice. What's more: even at double the volume, it will feel *easier* than it does now.

Instead of growing your practice the painful way you've always assumed you'd have to—by a pound of your flesh and hour after hour of your own time—you're going to learn a new way, a better way, that allows you to do more, give more, love more, serve more, accomplish more, and make more.

At the very core of this system is the fundamental premise of this book: **You can build a Remarkable Practice as Part of a Remarkable Life, not instead of one**.

You do this by making the fundamental shift from **owning a job to owning a business**.

"But I already *do* own a business!" you argue. Technically, that may be true. In a literal sense, yes, you may own your practice. But ask yourself this question: do you really own it or does it own you?

Let's say you didn't show up on Monday, would anybody notice? If your answer is "holy crap, yes, the place would screech to a halt" then that's called owning a *job*. And it's especially true if you're a single operator, the only doctor in your practice, which most chiropractors are. If you fall into that category, guess what? When you're not there, no doctoring is happening, no services are being rendered, and no money is being made.

## *Do you own a business, or do you own a job?*

Don't get me wrong, I know that you love your work, and you love the job. You may even be "successful" at running your practice, but the reality is most likely that the practice is running you. And if you're not careful, it will run you into the ground. The consequences are real and serious: burnout, injury, illness, divorce, and worse.

So how can you do it? How can you serve your Purpose, realize your Vision, build your "successful practice"—*and* avoid this pain? How do you build a Remarkable Practice as **Part** of a Remarkable *Life*? How do you go from owning a job to owning a business? That's the gap we are going to fill with this book.

This is the key—the difference between a job and a business is this:

## *Businesses are Scalable, Durable, and Transferable.*

You cannot build a Remarkable Practice as Part of a Remarkable Life if your practice does not have those three essential qualities.

First, your practice must be: **scalable**, which means that you can do more, serve more, love more, and make more, but it does not all have to be done by you. Real businesses do not run on "brute force"—they do not require a pound of your flesh and an hour of your time. Businesses run and build through **leverage**. By leveraging other people, systems, and technology, you can make a bigger impact *and* a better income, without it all having to be done by *you*.

Second, your practice has to be **durable**, which means that you can do more, serve more, love more, and make more even in your *absence*. This is what gives you the freedom to be able to build your Remarkable Life. Imagine being able to be home for dinnertime, bath time or at least bedtime. How about taking a few vacation weeks away from your practice without the place grinding to a halt? Like I said, the ultimate question is if you were to not show up on Monday morning would anyone notice? Now it's not that you don't want to show up—it's that you don't *have* to. We all know the difference.

Finally, your practice must be **transferable**, which means "saleable." Have you built your practice to sell it? I know that you may be thinking that you are far from worrying about selling your practice. You may even be thinking that you will never sell it—they will drag your carcass out of there in the end. But trust me—one day you will want to sell. You should be able to get paid handsomely for your practice—if it is a business. If someone could look at your practice and see that it was built like a real business, buyers would compete to buy your practice. You need an Exit Strategy. Your goal is to make a graceful and profitable exit. If you have been running a "job," you will find the eventual sale of your practice to be a painful experience.

It is a shame to see a practice retire with the doctor. Wouldn't it be better if you had a great DC come in as a successor and continue to care for your beloved patients? To continue your work and your legacy. And to have created a real business where your Team can continue to serve the Mission.

And the truth is, you will never regret building a practice to sell it. This "culture" creates a fantastic environment to work in and to own. Building a practice as a business from the start is the best approach, but even if you are years into the game, it's not too late to make this change. Better to do it now before you are trying to find a buyer.

## THE FOUR SEASONS OF THE CHIROPRACTIC CAREER

We've identified the Four Seasons of the Chiropractic Career:

*Launch, Build, Scale, and Exit.*

**The Launch Phase** consists of roughly your last year of school and your first year of practice. This is the season where you are just trying to figure it out. You are learning how to be a chiropractor—learning how to do the doctoring, the adjusting, and the patient education. You are focused on office location, layout, and office flow. You are trying to land on the systems that you are going to use to run the operations of your practice—and trying different approaches to your marketing (Attraction), sales (Conversion) and service/value delivery (Retention). And, of course, you are getting your first taste of hiring people and becoming a team leader.

The next season is **The Build Phase** of your career. You have established your physical plant and layout. You've created systems for Attraction, Conversion and Retention. You've hired employees. You are mastering chiropractic, adjusting, and patient education. You've settled into your role as entrepreneur and you're growing a busy practice. You are head-down and bum-up adjusting patients. You are most likely running your practice on brute force. You may be "successful," but you likely feel out of balance at home or out of shape or out of time. You are making a difference with your work and making some money, but you know that any additional growth would simply mean more imbalance, more time, and more overwhelm. You are experiencing some level of success—but, you are doing all of the work. God forbid, anything ever happened to you. You know that you are exposed. No one could do what you do. You are an Owner Operator. And you own a job.

Ideally, the next season is **The Scale Phase** of your career. This is where you realize that you can do more, give more, serve more, and make more, but it does not all have to be done by you. You begin to use leverage to build and run your business. You learn to leverage other people, systems, and technology. You've turned your job into a business. And you've transformed yourself from the Owner Operator to the CEO.

The final season for the DC is **The Exit Phase**. This is where the doctor/owner is ready to sell the practice and move into the next chapter of their life. And hopefully, you have prepared for this season. If you have, you have built a saleable asset. You have created a business that someone could see the value of, want to buy, and successfully build into the future. You have set yourself up for a graceful and profitable exit. Your successor can take over, continue to care for your patients, your Team can continue to serve the Mission—and it will be business as usual.

Unfortunately, most chiropractors run their careers like it's a hockey game, and there's only three periods to play: Launch, Build and Exit. All too often, chiropractors spend their entire career stuck in the Build Phase—and then abruptly find themselves at Exit—without having planned or prepared for it. This does not end well. They cannot find a successor. They cannot find a buyer. They panic, fire-sale or worse—the practice retires with them.

This does not have to be you.

Think of your career as a football game, and there are four quarters to play: Launch, Build, Scale and Exit. Regardless of where you are in practice today, let's make sure that you optimize your impact, experience, and outcomes. Let's get you into Scale. Let's turn your job into a business, and let's begin your transformation from Owner Operator to CEO.

This is the key to creating a Remarkable Practice as *part* of a Remarkable *Life*...not instead of one.

*The 4 Seasons of the Chiropractic Career*

## 4 SEASONS OF THE CHIROPRACTIC CAREER

| | REMARKABLE OWNER OPERATOR | | REMARKABLE CEO | | |
|---|---|---|---|---|---|
| **CONTEXT** | **LAUNCH!** | **BUILD!** | **SCALE!** | **EXIT!** | **SEASON** |
| **COMMUNITY** | ◉ In School Or First Year Out<br>◉ Find / Build Out A Practice<br>◉ Learning How To Doctor<br>◉ Building Clinical Skills<br>◉ Building Communication Skills<br>◉ Exploring / Developing Systems<br>◉ Learning How To Hire People<br>◉ Learning How To Market<br>◉ Trying To Establish A Tribe<br>◉ Just Trying To Figure It Out | ◉ Physical Office Established<br>◉ Systems Established<br>◉ Mastering Chiropractic<br>◉ Mastering Entrepreneurial Role<br>◉ Hired Employees<br>◉ Owner Operator<br>◉ Successful – But Still Own A Job | ◉ Leveraging Systems<br>◉ Leveraging Team<br>◉ Leveraging Training<br>◉ Leveraging Associate(s)<br>◉ Job Is Now A Business | ◉ Ready To Plan For Successor<br>◉ Want Graceful Exit<br>◉ Want Profitable Exit<br>◉ Want To Capture Value<br>◉ Patients Well Cared For<br>◉ Team Looked After<br>◉ Business As Usual<br>◉ Mission Continues | **CHARACTERISTICS** |
| | **START A PRACTICE** | **OWN A JOB** | **OWN A BUSINESS** | **CREATE A LEGACY** | |
| **CONVERSATION** | ◉ Don't Know What You Don't Know<br>◉ Lack Systems (Att/Conv/Ret)<br>◉ Don't Know How To Hire<br>◉ Lack Certainty<br>◉ Lack Conviction<br>◉ Lack Clarity<br>◉ Out Of Balance<br>◉ Own A Job | ◉ Struggling To Build A Team<br>◉ Capacity Issues<br>◉ Balance Issues<br>  ○ Schedule<br>  ○ Vacation<br>◉ High Exposure<br>◉ Not Scalable<br>◉ Not Durable<br>◉ Not Transferable<br>◉ No Exit, Stuck | ◉ Busy But Not Busy Enough<br>◉ Finding / Keeping "A Players"<br>◉ Finding / Keeping Great Associates<br>◉ Optimizing Associates (Effectiveness)<br>◉ Optimizing Systems (Efficiency)<br>◉ Resistance To Scaling<br>◉ Delegation / Trust / Control Issues<br>◉ Overwhelm<br>  ○ Team<br>  ○ Personal<br>◉ Still Owner Operator | ◉ You Own A Job<br>◉ Personality Based<br>◉ Business Is In Head<br>◉ Memory Management<br>◉ Systems Ill-defined<br>◉ Not Saleable / Transferable<br>◉ No Candidate For Successor<br>◉ No Idea How To Find One<br>◉ No Idea How To Sell / Exit | **CHALLENGES** |
| **CONTENT** | **TRP ACADEMY** | | **REMARKABLE CEO ACADEMY** | | **RESOURCES** |
| | **CHIROPRACTIC OPERATING SYSTEM** | | | | |

# WHO AM I?

I am a chiropractor from Boston, Massachusetts. I've had the privilege of checking spines and changing minds for over twenty years. I love chiropractic, and I love chiropractors. In fact, I married mine, Dr. Camilla Franson. I have seven chiropractors in my family. Both of my wife's sisters are chiropractors and both of them are married to chiropractors. My brother is also married to a chiropractor. We are like the Chiropractic *Cosa Nostra*.

For years, I was a burnt-out, overwhelmed, exhausted, "successful" chiropractor. (Or at least everyone around me thought I was successful.) I had all the outward signs of success: busy practice, big house, and lots of toys. But man, I was smoked.

Although we were helping lots of people, I felt like I was carrying the whole practice on my back. Really bench pressing the place every week. I was a horrible combination of "control freak" and perfectionist. And, I wanted to "do it all myself." I was a total Clydesdale Chiropractor.

I didn't know what to do. I was conflicted because I wanted to keep serving my purpose and growing my practice, but I knew that any growth simply meant more work for me. I was already so out of balance at home, falling out of shape, and just not having fun anymore—in the practice or in my personal life. Truth be told, I was stuck.

I was unsatisfied with where I was but afraid that it would be worse if I became even more "successful." I was running the practice on brute force. Just herding cats. Between my team and my patients, I couldn't even imagine doing more.

I started to question my Vision and my Purpose. My dirty little secret was that I didn't really want to grow the practice anymore. It would have just meant more work, more time, more energy, and greater imbalance in my life.

But then I experienced a breakthrough. At a low point and moment of feeling totally defeated, I asked myself, "What do I LOVE about our practice and why? Where specifically are things going smoothly, and why are they flowing there and not elsewhere?"

For us, the place we were seeing great results and having the most fun was on the clinical side. As practicing Gonstead doctors, we had the Gonstead Systems of analysis—the X-ray system, case management system, adjusting system. Everything was systematized. These repeatable systems that create **predictable** positive outcomes, over and over again. These reproducible systems created efficiency and results.

Most important, these systems created **Certainty, Conviction, and Clarity**.

I knew that I wanted those three things in *every* aspect of the practice: New Patient Attraction Systems, Conversion Systems, Retention Systems, Team Training Systems, you name it.

I started to realize that systems were the key to our **freedom**, and by systematizing every aspect of our practice, I could delegate and train my team to help me. I could continue to grow and, most important, *get my life back.*

From there I developed reproducible systems for every aspect of the business. I recruited and trained our team. The next thing I knew, our practice had tripled. But more important, we got our lives back. All of us did. We found our freedom in systems.

Creating systems came naturally for me, so much so that I'm now known as the systems guy. But it was a struggle at first to get over my inability to delegate. To this day, I consider myself a recovering control freak.

But once I became a **master systems creator, master delegator,** and **master trainer**, deep down I knew I could never go back. Once I gave myself permission to let go and delegate, it was like the seas parted—and now, with this book, I am giving *you* permission.

No, it's more than that: I am not just giving you permission to delegate, **I am *insisting* on it**. In order to free yourself up and do your best work, you must systematize, and then delegate. Trust me: it changes everything. You'll wonder what took you so long!

In our case, after making these changes, soon our practice grew to over 1,000 patient visits a week. And the quality of care, and the quality of our relationships with our patients improved incredibly. Patients got educated. Patients got great results. And, as the old adage says, "They stayed, paid and referred." Our Patient Retention was incredible. For example, our PVA or patient visit average was over 300 visits—that means that the average patient that started with us stayed for over 300 visits. And this was sustainable. We kept up those numbers for over fifteen years!

How did we do it? Being owner of this robust practice gave me a front row seat to what works and what doesn't. In the following chapters, I will break it all down step by step so that you can do it too.

I've been exactly where you may be now. I've felt lost and stuck, but I came out the other side. Since then, I've taught thousands of people how to build their own Remarkable Practice as Part of a Remarkable Life. Today, I spend most of my time training, equipping, and developing some of the world's top chiropractors and chiropractic teams.

I use the skillset that I honed over the past two decades, during which time I started four multimillion-dollar businesses. My first company took fifteen years to reach the million-dollar mark, but now it does a million dollars a month. The second company took ten years to reach a million dollars. With the third company, it took only five years—and the fourth company, two-and-a-half.

What accounted for that acceleration? I got better at it, and I did that by applying a very specific **system**. There's a system to creating a truly successful business (one that you would want to own and run). I discovered this system through trial and error—extracting these lessons from not only my successes but also my failures.

I am grateful for whatever success I've enjoyed; I believe that every business you launch is like going to school. But to be honest, I failed at least twice as many initiatives over that same period, and as much as I learned from the success stories, I learned plenty more from the failures.

> *Failure is not the opposite of success. It's* part *of success.*

It's "win or learn," as they say in the Navy SEALs. Ultimately, I took the lessons from both my successes and my mistakes, and I used them to "solve the puzzle."

Now I am sharing everything that I learned along the way with you in this book—my system for winning at business.

## SOLVING THE PUZZLE

How do you solve the puzzle of business success? Of practice success? Well, first it's important to recognize that what we're talking about here is not simply a one-dimensional puzzle like a jigsaw puzzle. I wish it was that easy. Rather, it's more like a Rubik's Cube.

As you know, the Rubik's Cube has six sides and you must solve all six sides together to really solve the puzzle. This is the perfect metaphor for your practice. As with a Rubik's Cube, your business has many facets. And like the cube, you can't solve the puzzle of practice success without solving—and maintaining—all six sides. And, if you screw up just one side, it jacks up the whole thing!

Like the Rubik's Cube, the system I teach and put forth in this book has six sides. Each of these "sides" needs to be solved. Here are the six sides of the puzzle:

1. **Vision**
2. **Leadership**
3. **Systems**
4. **People**
5. **Training**
6. **Energy**

In fact, I will suggest that they need to be "solved" in this order.

We will unpack each of these in the following chapters, but for now, here is a high-level view of each:

1. The first is **Vision**. Every great business starts with a compelling "Vision Story" that answers the question: "What does success look like to you?" Exactly what are you trying to accomplish? What does the better tomorrow that you are going to create look like?

2. Then next side is **Leadership**: Who do you need to become as a leader? What's the next best iteration of you? What qualities, attributes, behaviors, and skills do you need to develop to predictably attract, manifest, and lead your Vision?

3. The third is **Systems**: If you want to own a **business** instead of a job, you must systematize *everything*. Every core process

of your business must be systematized, including: Attraction Systems (New Patient Marketing), Conversion Systems (sales), Patient Retention Systems (Creating and Delivering Value and Service)—and maybe most important, Team-Building Systems.

4. Which leads us to the fourth side of the cube: **People**. Team building means knowing how to attract great talent, interview them, and hire them. You then need to know how to train them, develop them, and retain them. Assembling and keeping a great Team around you may be the single-most challenging *and* important piece of the business puzzle.

5. Then there is **Training** (fifth side): To win in business you must master onboarding new Team members, setting clear Expectations and Agreements, equipping them for success, and continually developing them as contributors and as people.

6. The sixth and final side of the cube is **Energy**. As we see throughout the book, energy is *everything*. Your practice is simply a reflection of your energy—your energy and your team's energy. When your energy is up, your practice is up. When your energy is flat, your practice is flat. When your energy is down, your practice is down. Your practice is an energetic organism. Energy is like sunbeams. You must decide exactly where you want the "fire" to start. As the CEO (Chief Energy Officer) of your practice, you must collect and direct your Team's energy. You must tell them *What's Important Now* and *What's Important Next* (W.I.N./W.I.N.) What do you need to focus on as a team, as a business? Focus is critical. Focus makes the difference between "busy-ness" and productivity.

So there you have it, my methodology for creating a Remarkable Practice as Part of a Remarkable Life. It's straightforward and it works. It sounds simple because it is. But it is *not* easy. This book will make it easier.

In the following chapters, I will walk you through everything you need to know to solve each side of this puzzle. For those who wish to dig deeper, there will be links to online references, tools, exercises, and other useful resources.

But it all starts with looking inward at what success looks like *for you*. That means establishing your **Vision Story**. Your unique vision for your success—a vision that's genuine and authentic to you, rooted in what's truly most important to you: your **Core Values**.

In the following chapter, you will gain **clarity** on these two critical elements: your Vision Story and your Core Values. They are the twin engines of success. Clarity is the greatest accelerant. Like gasoline on a fire, clarity accelerates everything. Lack of clarity creates friction and slows you down. If you get these right, everything will get easier. Everything will grow faster. You will have less stress, confusion, and anxiety, and you'll have more certainty, confidence, and peace. Let's get started.

> *Clarity is the Greatest Accelerant.*

## SUMMARY

- Objective: To Create a Remarkable Practice as Part of a Remarkable Life—not instead of one.
- You must turn your Job into a Business.
- Businesses are Scalable, Durable and Transferrable.
- You must solve the six sides of the Rubik's Cube of Practice Success:
  - Vision: What does success look like to you?
  - Leadership: Who do you need to become to lead this Vision?
  - Systems: All Core Functions of Business have to be systematized.
  - People: Surrounding yourself with A-Players is critical.

- Training: Invest in Training, Equipping and Developing your people.
- Energy: As CEO (Chief Energy Officer) you must clarify for your Team "What's Important Now" and "What's Important Next (W.I.N./W.I.N.)."

# CHAPTER ONE

# VISION

*"Be careful of how you define success, because
you're going to spend a lifetime pursuing it."*
—Pastor Bruce Boria

When I came out of chiropractic school, I thought I had a good idea of what "success" looked like: a big, busy practice. Inspired by countless mentors and legends, we were sure that bigger meant better—and success meant "busy!" Armed with what I believed was true clarity, I went to work, alongside the best and most invested partner I could have hoped for—my wife, Camilla.

Camilla and I met at Life University (at the First Quarter Party—a great story for a different book). We were broke students, so we spent a great deal of time at home on "date nights" visioneering our practice, eating homemade pizza or tuna fish sandwiches. We did an associateship in Virginia to hone our clinical skills and continued to spend hours designing our "dream practice" which was being built in Boston. We painstakingly designed every aspect of the practice and worked diligently to convey the details of our Vision to the team of builders six states away. Remarkably we built the whole thing remotely, and this was back in the pre-internet days when we were still drawing everything out on graph paper and sending faxes. I have vivid memories of driving down to Staples, paying two bucks per fax, going back and forth with the architects, hammering out what I wanted for every square inch of space.

But we had not just visioneered the physical plant—we had a clear vision for our Team, our patients, the equipment, the music, the posters, the energy...everything. All with extraordinary detail and intention. Clarity. We were going to build a busy practice!

The end result was exactly as we had imagined. It all started just as we had hoped: the physical space, then the patients, the team, everything. We had taken a super clear vision and manifested it. Our plan was actually working!

We were jamming. Yes, we were working crazy hours, skipping meals, workouts, and date nights, but we were building a practice. And a "successful one" at that. Everything was going beautifully...

Until we got north of about 350 patient visits a week.

Once we hit that threshold, everything started to break down. And I do mean everything, including our health, happiness—our whole lifestyle. I realized that although we had been operating with extraordinary clarity around how we wanted to build a busy practice, we had completely neglected creating a vision for our *life*—and how the practice was going to be a big part of our life.

I suddenly realized that I wanted it to be just that, a *part* of my life, not my whole life.

Camilla and I came to a shocker of a realization. We had let other people define success for us. We had almost literally borrowed someone else's definition of success, what it meant and looked like to *them*—not us.

So this left us with an incredibly important question: **what was *our* Vision of success?**

Amazingly, we had never really thought about it in that way. We just assumed that "success meant busy and busy meant success." What we had created was awesome—in a vacuum. We were helping a lot of people and serving our community. But it was at the expense of our health and happiness. What's worse, is that it wasn't sustainable, either. So that success was not going to last anyway.

The root of the problem was that we neglected to define success *for us* in light of *our* Core Values. In fact, our picture of success at the time was in many ways incongruent with what we believed in, because it failed to take into account what we held to be most important.

My frustration, my breakdown, was clearly rooted in this fundamental problem, this borrowed definition of success. I had taken on the trappings of everyone else's vision, and now I was paying the price.

## COMING TO CLARITY

Nothing is more important than having an authentic Vision for what success means to you. In order to arrive at that, you must be clear on what's most important to you—your Core Values. Core values are the fundamental beliefs of a person or organization. These guiding principles dictate behavior and can help people understand the difference between right and wrong.

I cannot and will not tell you what "success" looks like, but I will give you an operational construct:

> *Success is when you can achieve* alignment *between your Core Values, your Vision Story, and your Behaviors.*

Once you have true clarity around your Core Values and your Vision Story, the sky's the limit. The more clarity, the faster you're going to manifest what you want.

Clarity is "the greatest accelerant." It's like gasoline on a fire. But by the same token, when we *lack* clarity, it's a hindrance. It creates friction, interference, resistance. It slows us down. Too many chiropractors, and too many people in general, are held back by a lack of clarity. I see this as a root issue for so many of the thousands of DCs that I have coached.

Moreover, the only way to get to true clarity is to go through a process of unearthing. It's an inside-out process where we dig deep within ourselves to excavate our own definition of success. We do that by looking at what I call the twin engines of success, our "Vision Story" and our "Core Values." Those are the two most important factors. We must have a Vision Story that is aligned with our Core Values. This may seem obvious, but it's the very opposite of what most of us do, which is let someone else—from the outside—define what success looks like for us.

Fortunately, we can break this pattern and embrace a new **Inside-Out** paradigm. As we will see in this chapter, by sitting down and getting real with ourselves, and getting in touch with what's really important to us, we unearth an exciting new Vision Story—based, maybe for the first time in our lives, on what we *really* want.

Welcome to the first side of the Rubik's Cube of success: Vision.

> **The twin engines of success are your
> Vision Story and your Core Values.**

## WHAT IS A VISION STORY?

Simply put, the Vision Story is what success looks like for *you*—but put in the form of a story, not a statement. It's not the same thing as a Purpose Statement or Mission statement.

Your Purpose Statement answers the question: why are you here? Your Mission Statement answers the question: what are you going to *do* to serve your Purpose. Your Vision Story is a movie script. It's a saga...a blockbuster describing your Success Story...it's the story that describes the dent you are going to make in the universe. It's what you see when you close your eyes and envision the better tomorrow that you are going to create.

What does this vision of success look like for your practice, for your business, for your community, for your life?

If you do your job well, if you serve your Purpose and manifest your Vision, *this* is what it's going to look like, sound like, smell like, taste like. Think of your Vision Story as a movie script, for a movie called, *My Success Story*. You are the hero of this story, and you're going to have to ask a movie producer to cut you a check for $25 million to make the film—so you better tell it in as clear and compelling a way as you can! More on that in a moment.

But before you start to create your Vision Story, there is a very important thing you need to do first—let's identify your *Core Values*.

## YOUR CORE VALUES

What are the things in life that are most important to you? The answers to that question represent your Core Values—which are the basis for deciding how you choose to invest your time, energy, focus, and money.

To give you an idea of how this works, I will share with you my own Core Values. First there are what I call my "Core Four:" faith, family, fun, and health. For me, those are the granite blocks. And I lean on those to make some of the most important decisions in life.

But beyond my Core Four, I draw from some additional Core Values to help me with my daily decision-making around how I spend my time, energy, focus, and money. For sake of illustration, my other Core Values are: freedom, peace of mind, abundance, significance, and contribution.

Now, as helpful as these values have been in guiding my path, there have also been times when the individual values have competed with one another. Recognizing the ways that they clashed actually helped me reorganize my list. I used to have it in a slightly different order, with abundance before peace of mind. But then I switched those two, with peace of mind in front of abundance. What made me change?

Abundance—which most people think of as material wealth, and that is how I am using it here—has indeed always been very important to me. I've always been a guy who knows how to make money. When business challenges arise, I remain confident in my ability to just get to work and figure out a way to bring in more revenue.

My wife, on the other hand, is more concerned about peace of mind than she is about abundance. She is more risk-averse; I am more risk-tolerant. My mentality is *let's start a business, let's buy that property, let's invest in that company...if it doesn't go well, no matter, we'll take our hits, we've still got two other things going on, it's all part of the game.*

To which she would respond, "Well, Stephen, it's not part of my game."

Peace of mind is such a strong core value for Camilla that it basically supersedes my high priority on chasing abundance—and becomes the *family* core value. I recognize that her peace of mind is really important in our household, and therefore it is hugely important to me as well.

Moreover, by having established our core values—and by constantly evaluating and prioritizing—we can draw on them when an opportunity comes up. We can sit down together and ask ourselves, "Is this going to bring us toward freedom or away from freedom? Is it going to bring us peace of mind?"

Often there will be opportunities that will bring you toward abundance, but *at the expense of* freedom and peace of mind. Which is why it's so important to know yourself and your core values.

It's also important to distinguish between your ideal core values and how you actually live out those values in practice—or don't. There's often a big difference between what you wish your core values were and how you actually invest your time, energy, focus, and money.

Moreover, what would your spouse say your core values are? Is it different than what you put down yourself? What would your kids say? What about your best friends, the people who know you best, or the people who work most closely with you in your job?

It's always a good idea to run your core values by your closest people. Tell them, "These are what I think my core values are. I'd love for you to give me your thoughts and whether you think I'm living in line with these values or not."

This part of the process is the hardest—examining our **behaviors**. How we choose to invest our time, our energy, our money, and our focus.

Can those that are closest to you tell what your Core Values are based on your behaviors?

If this exercise feels unnerving, you're not alone. But uncovering contradictions is key to this process. If you don't, or if you choose to ignore the contradictions, you'll just continue on a path that leads to breakdown. As my friend, Dr. Pat Gentempo, puts it, "Contradiction leads to destruction."

*Contradiction leads to destruction.*

You need to make sure that your stated Core Values are true for you. I know that it's scary. The good news is that you only need to come up with these once—but you'll review them and reference them regularly. For readers who want or need more guidance, I have created this helpful worksheet and video: theremarkablepractice.com/vision.

## CREATING YOUR VISION STORY

Once you've identified your Core Values, then you can create your vision for what success looks like. It's time for you to write your Vision Story for the Remarkable Life that you want to live.

But remember: this only works if your Vision Story is in **alignment** with your Core Values. Where you have alignment, you will have peace and success. Where you have contradiction, you'll have stress and friction.

Don't worry: what you write is not set in stone. Your Vision Story is meant to be **dynamic**. It is going to change as you go through different stages of your life. Anybody who's been married, had children, started a business, or other such milestones, will know what I mean when I say there are different chapters in life, and your vision of success is going to change as you move through them.

So relax. Your Vision Story is a living document that you will continue to work on. Have fun with it. Again, this is your chance to be the hero of your own movie script for the success story of your life. Make it compelling. And make it clear. You want it to be understood by others and inspire them to join your team and get on board with your vision.

But that doesn't mean you're trying to appeal to everybody. Don't be afraid to be polarizing. Your Vision Story should be authentic to you. As such, it should compel some people to join you and repel others.

Your Vision Story will resonate with some people and not with others. And that's fine. If articulating them makes a member of your team say, "Whoa, I can't get behind that Vision Story, I'm outta here," so be it. In fact, it's for the better. Let's face it, even when everyone on your team is aligned, this is still hard. The last thing you need is someone in your boat rowing in the wrong direction.

Be vigilant in crafting your Vision Story. Make it authentically yours— and base it on what is truly important to YOU. Do not let other people project what success means on you. This vision will be the blueprint for your life. As my pastor, Bruce Boria once said, *"Be careful how you define success, because you're going to spend a lifetime pursuing it."* What we are after here is an unearthing of our Vision Story of Success—this is a true inside-out experience: http://theremarkablepractice.com/Vision.

## THE GOAL IS ALIGNMENT

As stated earlier, the premise of this book is for you to create a Remarkable Practice as *Part* of a Remarkable Life, not *instead* of one. So make sure that when you're crafting your Vision Story, you're thinking about it from a holistic perspective. It's not just about your practice. There are many sides to life—your spiritual life, mental, physical, relational, professional, etc.

Ideally, you want to have a Vision Story for each part of your life: a vision for your marriage, your role as a parent, your finances, your health, etc. These all get **integrated** into your overall Vision Story—your personal Success Story.

I know it can feel like a lot to think about it, but remember, nobody's asking you to be perfect. Remarkable does not imply perfect.

> *Remarkable does not imply perfect.*

These days it seems that everyone is chasing a kind of "perfect balance." Talk of "work/life balance" is all the rage. Honestly, I believe that **balance is bullshit**. Balance, in itself, is a terrible goal. If you are trying to live a life of significance, trying to have all the categories of your life perfectly balanced just doesn't work. Chances are that if you're living a life that's purposeful and aligned with your Vision Story and Core Values, there are definitely going to be times when your life feels wildly out of balance. You must give yourself *permission* to accept that.

Most people, and definitely most entrepreneurs (business owners—especially chiropractors) will find themselves "out of balance" in various seasons of their career and in their lives. You are trying to build a practice, run a business, raise a Team, lead a tribe of patients *and* be a great spouse, parent, child, friend, leader, athlete...being "out of balance" is the natural state of every business owner *most* of the time. This is not a "probably." This is a **definitely**.

Balance is not a destination; it's a reference point. You should use balance much like a sailor uses the horizon. A sailor does not view the horizon as a destination; the horizon is a reference point that helps the sailor navigate the ship and get to where they want to go.

I do recommend that you *keep your eye on balance*, and be aware of where you're out of balance so that you can reconcile it in the future. But you're never going to eliminate those seasons of your life where you feel out of balance. Trying to stay "balanced" all of the time is a waste of energy and a selfish pursuit. (Remember, you're trying to save the planet.) What's important is that when you are in those turbulent waters of imbalance, you stay mindful and aware. You know that it is temporary and that you have a plan to reconcile the imbalance on the other side.

It's also critical to be in agreement with your spouse or partner or family that you're going to be out of balance for a specific time period in order to accomplish something worthwhile and specific that serves your Purpose and Mission. You must agree that life is going to be a bit lop-sided for a while, but it will be temporary. Everyone is on the same page.

If you approach life in this way, you won't always feel "balanced" but you will achieve something even greater: *harmony*. When all is said and done, the goal is not balance, but **alignment**.

> *The Goal: Alignment between your Core Values, your Vision Story, and your Behaviors.*

Remember, ultimately what we're after here is a healthy, happy, and fully integrated life—personally and professionally. A life that is fulfilling. Purpose-Driven and sustainable. A Remarkable Life.

## WHO DO YOU NEED TO BECOME?

Now take a step back and reflect on what you've achieved so far. You now have clarity on your Core Values (what's truly most important to you) and your Vision Story (what success looks like to you). If you have not yet done these exercises—this is a good time to get these on paper as the rest of this book—and your success—will be built upon these as a foundation. The next step is to get clear about you and your role as the **Hero** of your Success Story.

Your Vision Story is the foundation. It is an expression of your Core Values and your Purpose. You have internalized it and can tell the story with such detail, clarity, and passion that people can see it, hear it, feel it. They are moved by it, and they are compelled to help you create it.

This level of clarity is powerful. You now know what to focus on. Your Team knows what to focus on. Instead of just being busy, you can finally be truly productive.

> *Focus is what makes the difference*
> *between busyness and productivity.*

If you lack focus, it doesn't matter how "On-Purpose" you are or how strong of a work ethic you have. This is true for your Team, as well. The truth is, most people aren't lazy; they're just overwhelmed because they're running around trying to do everything. And this is especially true with entrepreneurs. As they say, entrepreneurs don't starve, they drown. They drown in busyness.

If you're like most chiropractors, you know exactly what I'm talking about. But clarity around your Core Values and your Vision Story will change all that. You now know "what's important now." You can make decisions faster. You now know what success looks like for you. So how do you get there? What comes next?

You must now turn your attention to yourself as a leader. Who do you need to become to be the Leader of your Vision Story? What *attributes* and qualities will you need to develop to be able to attract and manifest that Vision? What do you need to work on personally in order to become this **next best iteration** of yourself as leader? Who do you need to become?

In the next chapter, we look at Leadership and the attributes required of the leader you are trying to become—the kind of leader who will be able to predictably attract and grow and sustain your new Vision of Success for your practice and your life.

## SUMMARY

- Your Vision Story describes what success looks like to you.
- Your Vision Story must be a manifestation of your Core Values.
- Core Values are the things that are fundamentally most important to you.
- Your Behaviors are how you choose to invest your time, energy, focus, and money.
- Success exists when you have *alignment* between your Core Values, your Vision Story and your Behaviors.
- You get to be the Hero of your Success Story—the next iteration of you.
- Who do you need to become to lead your Vision?

*To Download All the Chapter Resources, Go Here:*
1. theremarkablepractice.com/vision

*To Learn More, Check Out These Remarkable Resources*
2. TRP Academy: theremarkablepractice.com/tbr-academy
3. TRP Private Coaching: theremarkablepractice.com/tbr-coaching
4. Remarkable Live Immersion Events: theremarkablepractice.com/tbr-events

*1*

*2*

*3*

*4*

# CHAPTER TWO

# LEADERSHIP

*"What would the Leader that I am*
*trying to become do right now?"*
—Dr. Stephen Franson

After launching my practice in Boston, I soon figured out that I hadn't become the Leader that I wanted to be. I knew I had to make some changes immediately—or I would be trapped in a job—with attachments that did not serve me, my Team or my patients.

I had become attached to people "liking me." This is a terrible place to lead from. I had to get myself out of the mindset of trying to be popular. I'm a personable guy, a likeable guy. At the risk of sounding cocky, I know I can get 300 people a week to *like me* and do what I tell them to do. But then what I have is nothing more than a "personality practice," which is very limited and definitely *not* a business.

**I now realize that people hire us for our expertise—but they pay us for accountability.** Patients —or "Practice Members"—aren't looking for another pal. They don't need a new friend. What they need is a coach, somebody who they can look up to as an expert and authority, and who will hold them accountable (to doing what they need to do to get the results they want).

As we learned in the introduction, there's a big difference between owning a business and owning a *job*. Running a personality practice is owning a job. I owned a job, and if you ever took me out of the equation, the business would be done. It was that simple.

I had a similar experience with my Team. What kind of relationship did I want to have with my employees? I'll suggest that you can have one of three relationships with your Team: you can be their Boss or their Friend—or their Leader. Pick one.

I had to ask myself, did I want to be their boss or their friend? I knew I didn't want to be anyone's boss. It's not that it made me uncomfortable, but it just didn't interest me. As with patients, trying to be a friend to my employees was a terrible place to try to lead from. I knew I had to let go of my attachment to wanting to be "liked" by my Team as well. What mattered was that they trusted me. I wanted them to trust and respect me as a leader.

I knew as a leader I had to change my attachment from wanting to be "liked" by my patients and my Team—to being "trusted." I knew that if people trust me, they will do what I tell them to do. I also knew that if they did what I told them to do, they would get the results that they wanted. **If you help people get the results that they want, they will love you.**

It may sound weird for a leader to place importance on being loved, but being loved and being liked are two very different things. Think about how we raise our children. We all want our kids to love us, but the reality is that there will be times that they're not going to like us very much. And that's fine. Right? In fact, I'm sure that most of you who are parents would agree that this can be very challenging, but is absolutely necessary.

Once I overcame trying so hard to be liked by my employees and patients, I was able to make a fundamental shift as a leader. I wish I had come to the realization sooner. I couldn't see it until I had the "oh crap" moment and saw that my leadership style was fundamentally limited. It had become a cultural problem, one that HAD to change if I ever wanted to make the shift in my practice from "job" to business. But once I made the change, it was a different world.

## WHO ARE YOU AS A LEADER?

I suspect many of my readers share the same blind spot I did when it comes to leadership. If you are trying to become the best leader that you can be—and you must, if you're serious about creating a real business—that means upping your self-awareness game. You must take your consciousness of your own self, your life, and your behavior to a new level.

Let's establish a clear vision of you as the **Hero of your Success Story**. What is the next best iteration of you?

Who do you need to become to manifest your Vision? Every great leader needs a vision. It's up to you to be that leader. Somebody has to do it; nobody's going to do it for you. At the end of the day, only you can lead your vision into the future.

*What is the next best iteration of you as a Leader?*

The vision phase described in chapter one was more introspective, but now's the time to go beyond and cast that vision outside of yourself. Who do you need to become in order to be the leader who can predictably create, attract, manifest, and lead that better tomorrow? Who do you need to become as a doctor? As a boss? As an educator, a clinician, a marketer?

What about as a role model? Are you practicing what you preach as a chiropractor, someone who teaches people about the wellness lifestyle and how to achieve optimal health? If you're going to talk the talk about the holistic approach toward a fully integrated life, you have to walk the walk. That means looking across your life and asking, "Who do I need to become in my fitness life? Who do I need to become in my spiritual walk? Who do I need to become in my relationships, my marriage, my role as parent? Who do I need to become financially?"

Then, you must become a good steward of *all* of these categories. Does that mean you're going to become a perfect human being overnight? Absolutely not. But this is a journey of **progression not perfection**. Again, remarkable does not mean perfect.

## THE LEADERSHIP MUSCLE

So where do you begin to solve this second side of the Rubik's Cube puzzle of success? What can you do now, starting today, to develop this leadership muscle?

First, take a moment to close your eyes and think about the following. Picture yourself as the kind of extraordinary leader of your practice who you're trying to become. What would *that guy* say and do right now? What kind of leader would he be? What would the doctor that I am trying to become do right now? What would she say?

Then, think about your personal life. The husband you're trying to become: what would he say and do right now? Think about the father that you're trying to become? What would he do? The mother I am trying to become: what would she do? What would the wife that I am trying to become…What would she say right now?

When I lead groups and have them do this exercise, often folks will come up to me afterwards and tell me how much they enjoyed it. In particular, they talk about how it had the effect of making them think about others, those leaders who they admire most: their role models.

Role models are indeed very important. One of my mentors, Dr. Guy Reikeman calls it your **Virtual Board of Trustees**—people who you can reference as exemplars of what it means to behave and act like a great leader categorically. That said, what's most important here is to think deeply about *yourself* and the changes you need to make to become the person you want to be.

Remember, this journey you are on—to creating a Remarkable Practice as Part of a Remarkable Life—is an *inside-out* process. There is nothing more powerful and compelling than when someone really embraces this exercise and goes deep inside; it's almost like they're looking at themselves as they really are for the very first time.

They examine the picture they see and come out of with all sorts of amazing insights: "I know I need to grow up, I know I need to be more mature, more patient, tender, empathetic." In some ways, it feels like they're bulldozing their old self to make room for the new. Now they know that the next best version or iteration of themselves as a doctor, for example, is going to be someone who's more patient or empathetic, or whatever the case may be.

If you allow yourself to go deep in this way, you will come out with the same kind of breakthrough. Pick the thing about yourself that you know is a bit of a handicap or hamstring. What is it that's holding you back right now as a leader? How does that piece look different on the future you?

As you follow this train of thought and develop this muscle, you'll begin to have a very clear and intimate relationship with this future you, this next iteration of yourself. You're creating a kind of familiarity with this (for now, imaginary) person, this doctor, leader, boss, husband, father—as a reference point—a True North. A true hero.

*What would the Leader that I want to become do right now?*

The more focused and clear that you can make the picture, the more concrete and actionable, the more success you'll have in accelerating your growth in becoming that individual in your mind's eye, that better leader—that next best iteration of you.

By constantly checking your behaviors and responses against that person you're trying to become, you'll start to grow more and more aware and **aligned** with these new standards you've set for yourself. You'll also have a greater awareness of when you may be acting out of integrity or alignment with the leader you are trying to become. Again, the goal is not perfection, **the goal is alignment**. Your behaviors are congruent with the image of what and who you're trying to become as a leader.

## CERTAINTY, CONVICTION, AND CLARITY

In order for you to become the leader you want to be—the kind of leader who will be able to create, attract, and lead your vision of success—you need to not only have a clear picture of that person but also the specific attributes that make them who they are.

*What are the leadership muscles that you need to build?*

In particular, I want you to consider the leadership qualities that I consider The Big 3: namely **Certainty, Conviction, and Clarity**. I'll suggest that these are the three "X Factors" of Chiropractic Success. Ask yourself, what level of Certainty are you going to need to develop to become the leader that you want to be? What level of Conviction, what level of Clarity?

Why are Certainty, Conviction, and Clarity so important? Having worked with thousands of chiropractors around the world, I've found that these are the common denominators of success. They are also the most common areas where doctors struggle. Within any practice, when you see success getting derailed, or when doctors are simply not realizing their full potential, chances are it's related to the doctor's lack of certainty, conviction, or clarity—or some combination of those.

Let's start with the first of these, **Certainty**, the state or quality of "lacking doubt." Certainty is a very attractive quality. People are drawn to certainty, especially when they're looking for a leader, a doctor, an expert. When we sense a real certainty in someone, it pulls us in and makes us trust them.

Communication experts say that 92 percent of communication is unspoken. People innately pick up on wishy-washiness or uncertainty. In fact, we're hardwired to run away from it; it's a survival mechanism. But by the same token, when we encounter someone who radiates real certainty, we run toward it. We can just feel it in the person. Instinctively, we relax and think to ourselves, "this guy knows what he's talking about" or "she knows what she's doing."

How does this manifest in a chiropractic practice? I've seen many doctors plagued by self-doubt: clearly they are experiencing issues around certainty or conviction, or both. Sometimes they're wishy-washy in telling their patients what to do, or they waver when giving them recommendations for care and the direction they need. Or maybe the doctor struggles with follow-through or has a problem keeping patients accountable.

Why are these docs so hesitant? I'll suggest that it is because they are not standing on a granite foundation of Certainty and Conviction.

What do we mean exactly by **Conviction**? I mean that the doctor truly "owns" their Recommendations for Care. The doctor truly believes that his or her recommendations are exactly what the patient needs to do to get what they want. Nothing more. Nothing less. When a doctor gives their recommendations for care with real conviction, the patients respond enthusiastically, "Yes, I'm in. I'm going to do it."

It's important to understand that conviction is a two-sided coin. On the one side, there's the doctor's conviction. The doctor has to genuinely believe that their recommendations are the best path for the patient to get the results they're looking for. Then, on the other side, there's the patient's conviction that they're in good hands, they're in the right place, and they've found the doctor who's going to help them get what they want.

What about **Clarity**? Challenges around clarity might be even more pervasive. Sometimes it seems like everyone struggles with this one. What does clarity look like in a chiropractic practice? Clarity is when you can tell patients *exactly* what to do and how to do it. Clearly tell them how to get the results that they want. When someone hires an expert, they want that expert to tell them exactly what to do. People love clarity. They are drawn to it. In fact, people are repelled by lack of clarity. Like the saying goes, "Confusion does not convert."

Humans in general are attracted to clarity and they are repelled by lack of clarity. It's innate. When somebody tries to give us direction and isn't clear about it, it's just frustrating and unproductive.

In any practice, when you have a leader who's not clear about what to do now and what to do next—and why it needs to be done and *how* it needs to be done— the leader will start losing their people, both their patients and their employees. No one wants to follow a leader who lacks clarity. You must create clarity around the **value** of staying.

Your patients need clarity to start care, for sure—but it is even more critical that they have clarity around the value of staying under care (more about that in the following chapter).

Patients drop out of care when they lack clarity—in other words, people leave when things get wonky.

## STOP DOING THIS. START DOING THAT.

Here's what I've seen: **your success is going to be limited by your weakest pillar**. Don't get me wrong. You may already be doing well in your practice. You may appear "successful" to everyone, just like I did. But chances are, you have a weak pillar when it comes to certainty, conviction, or clarity.

Even if you're a ten out of ten in two of those, but weak on the third, it's going to limit your success in creating a truly Remarkable Practice as Part of a Remarkable Life. To become the next best iteration of you as a Remarkable Leader—you must begin to reconcile this. The first step is to self-identify. What are my greatest strengths? And where are my points of exposure? The next step is to reconcile this exposure. Intentionally train the "leadership muscles" that you've left undeveloped or let atrophy—and build a Remarkable Team around you that brings their genius to the table. More on that in future chapters.

> *Your success is limited by your weakest pillar:*
> *Certainty, Conviction, or Clarity.*

We already know that contradiction leads to destruction, and that we want to change any behavior that contradicts our vision story and core values. So the first step is to recognize these behaviors for what they are and commit to changing them.

Toward this end, you must ask yourself, "What are the behaviors that you need to stop doing?" Everybody loves a to-do list. Think of this as your **"to-don't list."**

For example, as a chiropractic doctor, you really can't tell people not to smoke cigarettes if you still smoke yourself. That is obviously a contradiction. You can't tell patients they need to exercise regularly or get good sleep or reduce their stress if *you* are not practicing those healthy behaviors.

Next, ask yourself, "What are the behaviors that you need to *start* doing?"

Through this exercise and the other leadership exercises you've done in this chapter, you are well on your way now to understanding what your own best work looks like, and the best version of yourself as a leader. You know the attributes you need to focus on to become that person.

In the following chapters, you will see the importance of Certainty, Conviction, and Clarity as we learn to build systems around the three operational domains of our practice—the mechanisms for Attracting, Converting, and Retaining patients.

Here's what I know:

> *Attraction is a Reflection of your Certainty.*
> *Conversion is a Reflection of your Conviction.*
> *And Retention is a Reflection of your Clarity.*

Having identified the importance of these three—certainty, conviction, and clarity—you will discover in this book exactly what needs to be done to slay the dragons holding you and your practice back. Now you know the roots of the challenges you are experiencing. It's time to begin our journey of increasing *your* certainty, *your* clarity and *your* conviction, so that you can accelerate your success and create your own Remarkable Practice.

As the hero of your journey and your success story, you have reached the point where you turn your attention outward, to your business. In chapter one and two, you got clear on what success looks like for *you*, based on your core values, and who you need to become to lead this vision to fruition.

Now it's time to take what you've learned so far and apply it to your operations—and systematize it throughout your organization. It's time to talk **systems**, because systems are a critical factor in turning your job into a business.

## SUMMARY

- You need to become the Hero of your Success Story.
- As a leader, you should be attached to people trusting you—not liking you.
- You must develop the Leadership Muscles of Certainty, Conviction and Clarity.

## QUESTIONS

- Who do you need to become to lead your Vision Story?
- What attributes (Leadership Muscles) do you need to develop?
- What are your greatest strengths? Where are you exposed?

- What do you need to Start Doing to become the next iteration of you as a leader?
- What do you need to Stop Doing to become the next iteration of you as a leader?

*To Download All The Chapter Resources, Go Here:*
1. theremarkablepractice.com/leadership

*To Learn More, Check Out These Remarkable Resources*
2. TRP Academy: theremarkablepractice.com/tbr-academy
3. TRP Private Coaching: theremarkablepractice.com/tbr-coaching
4. Remarkable Live Immersion Events: theremarkablepractice.com/tbr-events

1      2      3      4

# SYSTEMS

*"Systematize everything."*

—Dr. Stephen Franson

If you were to ask me what differentiates owning a business from owning a job in just one word, that word would have to be "**systems.**"

Systems are what make your business **scalable**, **durable** and eventually—**transferable**. Systems create reproducibility. Systems create consistency. Systems allow you to delegate and equip you to train. Systems create leverage. If you want to own a business—you must create systems for everything.

As a Chiropractor, every core function of your practice must be systematized: Attraction (marketing), Conversion (sales), Retention (value creation and delivery) and Team Building (human resources and development).

In my early days of practice, when it came to operations, I used to make it up as I went. I was pretty good on my feet, and I got away with it for a while. But as the practice grew, this was unsustainable.

So how did I go from being the "King of Wing" to eventually becoming known as The Systems Guy?

It all changed when I recognized that I was building a practice that relied on **memory management and lots of horsepower—my horsepower**. As I said, this approach was effective initially, but eventually I was maxing out and stifling the growth of the practice. Ironically, it turns out that what had created a certain level of "success" in the practice to that point was exactly what was preventing the "business" from going to the next level. I was trying to remember everything about our practice, *everything* that I taught my employees and my patients. Eventually, the wheels started falling off the wagon.

Running my practice that way was stressful and inefficient. Using memory management and brute force takes a lot of mindshare and energy. It's exhausting.

But an even bigger problem was how my approach was leaving **knowledge gaps** in others. For example, when it came to Patient Education—the key to great Patient Retention—I was losing track of what I had taught each patient. Each human being, of course, is on his or her own journey of learning. As I accumulated more and more patients, I started to lose sight of where they all were in their journey, what each of them knew and didn't know.

I started making assumptions that I had taught them something that I hadn't or that they understood something that they really didn't. These "gaps" are like missing planks in a "hanging bridge" of patient education. Any missing plank creates a dangerous opening through which patients can fall and drop out of care. It was my responsibility to lead my patients and educate them and change the way they thought about their health.

If I couldn't do that, they would never change their behavior and therefore, their health wouldn't improve. And if our practice wasn't helping them get better health outcomes, what the hell were we doing here anyway?

I realized that it was critically important to pay attention to where a person is on their learning curve—what they've been told, what they've been taught, and what they *understand* at any given point. You just can't leave it to chance or memory management. Your Patient Education must be systematized.

For example, I realized that in order for patients to get better health outcomes, they had to change their behaviors. But I also learned that for their behaviors to change sustainably, they would need to change their **beliefs**. You see, our behaviors drive our outcomes, but our belief system drives our behavior. So in order to change someone's results, you must change their behavior. And in order to change their behavior, you must **change their minds**.

> *Beliefs organize Behaviors. Behaviors drive Outcomes.*

So I identified the twelve key things that I wanted my patients to know. I realized that if people understood these twelve concepts— these twelve simple things—they would change their behaviors and get better results. In fact, they would *understand*—and therefore never leave—chiropractic. My Associate Doctors called them **The Dirty Dozen**. (I had them written down on a piece of paper that had become worn and torn over the years of heavy use.)

We taught these twelve concepts over and over again throughout the first several months of every patient's care. They lived in the New Patient Consultation, Exam and Report Process, of course; but then got baked into every visit after that through continued Patient Education: in "Table Talk," the New Patient Orientation Workshop and in Progress Exams and Progress Reports.

If you went through our Patient Process—you learned The Dirty Dozen. No guessing. No memory management. No forgetting. It is a **system**.

For more on the Dirty Dozen, go here: <u>theremarkablepractice.com/ systems</u>.

You've got to know where they're at in every stage of the process and make sure that gaps don't develop inside your patient communications. Otherwise, you'll start to lose patients and see them drop out of communication altogether. Remember the premise: Retention is a Reflection of Clarity.

### *Your Retention Is a Reflection of Clarity.*

When it comes to your **Team** and **Operations**, you must systematize every step of every process so that you can *delegate* and *train*. You must define your process and procedures—and then capture it in writing. Like Dr. John Demartini says, "If it's not written down, it doesn't exist." You must have current Operations Manuals—The Playbook that everyone on your Team trains on and follows to the letter.

To truly build a business, you must **systematize everything**. Systems are the third side of the Rubik's Cube of Success. Having systems for

Operations, for example, means defining: *this is what we do and say on day one, this is what we do and say on day two, this is what we do and say on day three*...and so on and so forth, all the way through the lifetime of the patient.

Systematizing Operations is considered *table stakes* for turning your job into a business—it's an absolute nonnegotiable.

Think about capturing your process like writing a screenplay, and every step in your process is a scene in the play. For example, I think of the New Patient Conversion Process as "one communication" that takes place across three days. It's a story that the patient follows—and participates in. The first day is about **Connection and Discovery**. Day Two is all about **Ownership and Direction**. And Day Three is about **Expectations and Agreements**. We'll do a deep dive on each of these in the upcoming chapters.

We have systematized and documented every step of every process of every day. We have captured the intellectual property of our business: "this is what we do, how we do it, and what we say when we do it." If you want to grow your business without creating a bigger job for yourself, you need to do this for every operational domain of your practice: Attraction, Conversion, Retention, and Team Building.

On the following page is an excerpt from our Conversion Manual—Day One Process Flowchart. You can see our Remarkable Operations Manuals here: theremarkablepractice.com/tbr-manuals.

Think about your Team Trainings like the dress rehearsal of a play—every step in your Patient Process can be trained on, scene by scene. Now you and your Team may have gone through a "scene" a thousand times with a thousand different patients; but you must remember, it's the first time each New Patient is doing it. So stay focused and deliberate.

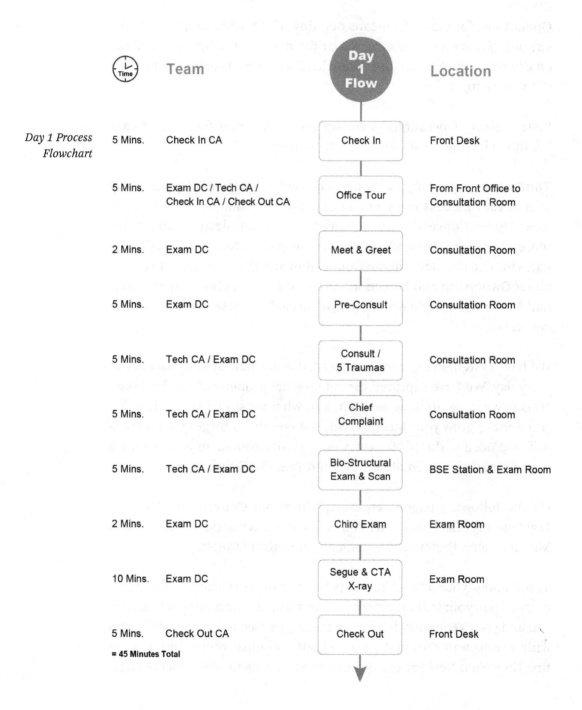

*Day 1 Process Flowchart*

| Time | Team | Day 1 Flow | Location |
|------|------|-----------|----------|
| 5 Mins. | Check In CA | Check In | Front Desk |
| 5 Mins. | Exam DC / Tech CA / Check In CA / Check Out CA | Office Tour | From Front Office to Consultation Room |
| 2 Mins. | Exam DC | Meet & Greet | Consultation Room |
| 5 Mins. | Exam DC | Pre-Consult | Consultation Room |
| 5 Mins. | Tech CA / Exam DC | Consult / 5 Traumas | Consultation Room |
| 5 Mins. | Tech CA / Exam DC | Chief Complaint | Consultation Room |
| 5 Mins. | Tech CA / Exam DC | Bio-Structural Exam & Scan | BSE Station & Exam Room |
| 2 Mins. | Exam DC | Chiro Exam | Exam Room |
| 10 Mins. | Exam DC | Segue & CTA X-ray | Exam Room |
| 5 Mins. | Check Out CA | Check Out | Front Desk |

**= 45 Minutes Total**

You will find that New Patients will bring to the table a thousand different variables of their own. **You and your Team have to show up as the constant.** That is why we train, so that you know your systems, your processes, and your procedures. If you train hard, and master your process, it will free you up to do what's most important with your patients: **staying present and focusing on them**. You'll be able to take them through the process and keep your mind entirely focused on that person in front of you, not yourself, and your team wondering what you should do or say next.

I love what the Navy SEALs say about training:

> *"Under pressure, you don't do what you know—*
> *you revert to what you've **trained** on."*

As we've now learned, processes and procedures get repeated over and over again with every patient. It's essential, therefore, that every part be written down and captured in a manual that team members can reference. This manual will become your gold standard of excellence and explain exactly how you do everything that you do.

When you start to think of your practice this way, you'll look at your business through a new lens. You'll begin to scrutinize every part of your practice—looking for processes and procedures that must be repeated consistently. If you want to increase efficiency, you'll need to systematize. If you want predictable outcomes—systems. And if you wish to create a business that is Scalable, Durable and eventually, Transferable—then everything must live as a system.

> *In order to make your practice Scalable, Durable, and*
> *Transferable…You must systematize everything.*

In the coming chapters, you will look across the whole landscape of your business with an eye toward systematizing. You will ask yourself: what are the core competencies of this business? What are the things that we do over and over again, which need to be performed consistently in order to have predictable, positive outcomes?

Never forget: you are in the business of saving lives. That's *why* you do what you do. That's why you fell in love with chiropractic in the first place. **And when business is good, everybody wins.** Isn't it time we started to act like that?

So with that in mind, let's tackle each domain of your practice together and systematize your operations. Let's take your job and turn it into a business.

But where do you start, you ask? Again, looking across the landscape of your practice, you will see four domains: **Attraction, Conversion, Retention, and Team Building.**

The first three are the fundamental elements of practice operations. Attraction means marketing and attracting new patients. Conversion is sales—converting potential new patients into active patients. Retention is creating and collecting ideal patients who will follow your recommendations, get great results, and stay under care. Team Building is its own animal. It is the X Factor that will drive or derail your business. It is such a significant element to business building that it gets its own side of the Rubik's Cube—and its own chapter in this book.

Let's recall from the end of chapter two several fundamental, operational constructs.

> *Your Attraction is a Reflection of your Certainty.*
> *Your Conversion is a Reflection of your Conviction.*
> *Your Retention is a Reflection of your Clarity.*

In the following chapters, we will unpack each of these and show you how to systematize each one. If you were to master even one of these domains, your practice would grow and flourish. Can you imagine what your practice—and your *life*—will be like when you master all three?

Let's begin with Attraction.

## SUMMARY

- You must systematize every Core Function of your business.
- Systems create reproducibility and consistency.
- Systems allow you to delegate and train.
- Systems create Scalability and Durability.
- Every step of your Patient Process and Procedure must be defined and captured (written down) in current and complete Operations Manuals (The Playbook).
- Systems create *leverage* and turn your *job* into a *business*.

*To Download All the Chapter Resources, Go Here:*
1. theremarkablepractice.com/systems

*TRP DC and CA Process and Procedure Manuals:*
2. theremarkablepractice.com/tbr-manuals

*To Learn More, Check Out These Remarkable Resources*
3. TRP Academy: theremarkablepractice.com/tbr-academy
4. TRP Private Coaching: theremarkablepractice.com/tbr-coaching
5. Remarkable Live Immersion Events: theremarkablepractice. com/tbr-events

*1*      *2*      *3*      *4*      *5*

# CHAPTER FOUR

# SYSTEMS OF ATTRACTION

> *"I will sell Chiropractic, serve Chiropractic, and save
> Chiropractic if it will take me twenty lifetimes to do
> it. I will promote it within the law, without the law, in
> keeping with the law or against the law in order to get
> sick people well and keep the well from getting sick."*
>
> —*B.J. Palmer*

I've talked to thousands of chiropractors over the years and the one thing that I hear from them all the time is, *"Man, if I just had more New Patients."* It doesn't matter whether their practice is brand new or they've been around for years, struggling or booming, it's always the same: *"I need more new patients."*

When I hear this from docs, I know that they are coming from a place of good intentions. The chiropractors I encounter tend to be very Purpose-Driven: they want to help more people and have a bigger impact.

Attracting more New Patients should always be Purpose-Driven. The most successful DCs that I know have this in common: they are looking for more New Patients out of inspiration—not desperation (to paraphrase John Demartini). They want to expand their reach and impact, not just replace patients that are dropping out of care (otherwise known as "replacients")—and, of course, increase their income. We all want to make a bigger income, and in my experience, that comes more readily when you focus on making a bigger impact.

If you find yourself plugging holes with *"replatients,"* I'd suggest that you change the way you think about the problem. I like to remind DCs that **there's no shortage of New Patients looking for help.** That is not the problem. Think about it: you've all heard the statistics about health issues in this country. Do you really believe there is a shortage of sick and suffering people out there right now looking for help?

Of course not. There is literally swarms of people all around you that are desperate, staying up late at night, popping pills, and Googling for answers to their health problems. They're asking their friends and family. They're walking into hospitals. They're going to Doc-n-the-Box. Going to emergency care centers.

So what we have to recognize first of all is that there's no shortage of New Patients. The truth is—they have you surrounded. There are thousands of people who are suffering and are *actively* looking for help. The question is...are they looking for *your* help.

Think about it. Health concerns—sickness, symptoms, crisis, conditions—are likely the dominant conversation going on all around you. At the beauty salon, the water cooler, the dentist chair, the Facebook feed...everyone's talking about health issues. **The problem is that *you're* not in the conversation.**

As an industry, *Chiropractic* is not in the conversation to the extent that we should be. Yes, as chiropractors we have potential New Patients all around us, but they're not looking to us for help. They're looking elsewhere, because we are not in the conversation that is already happening.

> ### *You have to get in the conversation.*

So how do we *get* in the conversation? How do we make ourselves relevant? That's where **marketing** comes in.

Remember: nobody's Googling "subluxation correction" and ending up in your office. They're not searching for "optimal health," "perfect posture," or "lifetime family wellness." What they *are* doing is looking for help with their health issues, whatever health crisis they may be going through, whether it's for them personally—or for their family or friends.

Are they going to find you?

But before we talk about *how* you get into *their* conversation, we have to address **who you are** when you do get into the conversation. Who you are when you show up will determine how effective you are when you get there. You must know why you are unique, what you offer, how you can solve their problem. But most of all, you must **show up to the conversation with *Certainty*.**

After all, the Purpose of any business is to **solve a problem**—to add value to a person or another business by solving a problem that they know they have. And you better show up with certainty around who you are, what you offer, how you solve their problem, and why someone should come see *you*.

I'll say it again:

> *Your attraction is a reflection of your certainty.*

The mechanism for attracting people is marketing. Effective marketing comes down to three things: Strategy, Tactics and Mindset. Strategy is your plan around what to do and *why* to do it. Tactics are about the things that you are going to do and *how* to do them. Mindset is all about *who* you are when you do all of the above.

But before we delve into the nuts and bolts of marketing, let's remember what we learned in chapter two about leadership: **Certainty is the most attractive quality in a leader.** And Attraction—attracting new patients through marketing—is a reflection of that certainty.

Let's first talk about your Mindset. Take a moment now to think about yourself. Where does your Certainty come from?

## THE FOUR PILLARS OF CERTAINTY

In my experience there are four primary sources of Certainty: Philosophical Certainty, Clinical Certainty, Communications Certainty and lastly, Certainty around Business Acumen.

**Philosophical Certainty** is like a superpower in our profession. In fact, I bet that when I even mentioned "certainty" you probably assumed that I meant Philosophical Certainty. Our philosophy serves as the foundation—the bedrock on which we build our careers. Our philosophy shapes our beliefs, drives our decisions, and determines our behaviors. Doctors who consider their Chiropractic Philosophy as their primary source of Certainty are typically emboldened and confident—and are usually highly magnetic and successful.

Doctors who love caring for patients, champion their technique, pride themselves on helping difficult cases, and thrive in the academics of the art and science of chiropractic will often find that **Clinical Certainty** is their primary source of certainty. These are the doctors who reek of confidence and competency. These are the doctors you would jump on an airplane to see if someone in your family was in crisis.

The third source of certainty is **Communications Certainty**. These chiros know that they can tell the story. They can tell the Chiropractic Story in such a compelling way that they can move people. They can make people take action. These doctors know that they can sit with an individual or stand in front of a room and get people to think differently and act differently. These docs are Rainmakers—they have Communications Certainty.

Finally, there are **Business Builders**. These doctors know that they can create a business out of vapor. They love the challenge of finding a location, closing a deal, designing a floor plan, creating operations systems, building a Team, training and leading that Team, marketing, and sales. They love to create value, deliver value, add value, and capture value.

> *The four pillars of certainty are philosophical certainty, clinical certainty, communication certainty, and business acumen.*

If you're not sure at first which kind of certainty fits you, think about it this way: you may be good at more than one, but I guarantee you one of them is your primary source of certainty. It's your Superpower.

Then, once you have identified and own that primary zone, go ahead and ask yourself, which of the four are you the weakest in? Where is the greatest opportunity for growth for you? If you can be honest with yourself here and identify the strong and weak pillars within you, you can make a plan to reconcile your weaker pillars.

Here's what I know:

> *Your success will be limited by your weakest pillar.*

All four sources work together, like muscle groups orchestrating complex patterns of movements in our bodies. Your clinical skills and philosophy drive your communications, which drive your business. If your business skills suck, then it's going to undermine the rest and distract you from delivering great care. If you know that your clinical skills are lacking—it will undermine your communications. If your communications are off, you'll derail your business success... and so on.

Long story short, if any of these four are sideways, it's going to have a derailing effect on your practice. But it's still important to identify your strongest pillar and spend most of your time there. Then, where you are weak, you must become very intentional about reconciling this in two ways:

1. Work on developing those weaker muscles to mitigate your exposure.
2. Build a Team around you that *collectively* is great at everything.

To work on yourself, you must work on each of these pillars like athletes train muscle groups: specifically and deliberately. How are you working on your philosophy? Your clinical skills? Your communication skills? Your business acumen? Who are you studying? What are you reading? What podcasts are you listening to? Who are you training with? Who is your coach? What seminars are you attending?

Also important, you must know where to look in terms of fleshing out your team with people who are really strong where you aren't as strong. For example, if Business Acumen is not your gift, you know you're going to need someone who's a good business strategist and coach.

You may need someone who is great at operations. You'll need a great bookkeeper and accountant, also someone who knows what needs to be in place as far as statistical tracking and reporting systems.

Now, this doesn't mean you can completely relegate those duties to someone else. You can't just say: *"Well, I don't care about all that stuff, you handle that."* If you do, it will come back to haunt you. Communication may not be your forte, for example, but you still need to know enough about your Market Message, for example, to guide the marketing expert you should hire.

Don't worry, you will get there. For now, you've zeroed in on your gifting and primary areas of Certainty—it's time for you to build on what you've discovered. Draw on whatever your strengths may be to put together your marketing plan for how to get yourself out there and become visible in the marketplace. We'll tackle fleshing out your Team in a separate chapter.

## YOUR MARKETING PLAN

When it comes to generating New Patient Leads, there are three kinds of marketing: **internal marketing, external marketing**, and **digital marketing**. Like all entrepreneurs, business owners tend to have *shiny object syndrome*. Whenever somebody comes up with something new, they abandon what they were doing before and try to reinvent the wheel.

Instead of doing that, I encourage you first to take a moment and assess what part of marketing you actually enjoy doing, If you love something, it means you're probably good at it. If you hate it, chances are you suck at it. Everybody's going to be different and that's OK. (Again, we will hire in and outsource others to leverage their gifts—but more on that in the Team Building chapter ahead.)

For example, I'm good at dinner talks, outside speaking events, and corporate wellness programs. I like to be in the front of the room. For others, that stuff is their worst nightmare. Maybe they're better at spinal screenings and health fairs, where they're working with the person one-on-one. Or maybe they're great at doing a Webinar or a Facebook Live, or writing white papers and social reports, or leading internal campaigns in their office (like Kid's Week or Valentine's week).

We all have our different strengths, and the good news is that there are so many effective tactics out there to choose from—and plenty of Perspective New Patients desperately looking for your help.

A good **Marketing Plan** begins by identifying the strategies and tactics that you are going to employ and committing them to a **Marketing Calendar**.

So take the time now to start writing out your business plan and marketing calendar. Again, there's no right or wrong here: you don't have to do *everything*.

What is important, however, is that all of your marketing efforts live on a calendar. That may seem obvious, but the point is that it commits you to a plan for the next twelve months. Your whole team can look at it and know: *these are the themes of the month, and this is where we're headed next*, etc.

> *You must have a marketing plan and you must have a marketing calendar.*

A best practice for an effective Marketing Plan is to adopt a theme for the year or season. Themes create focus and structure. And remember, focus is what makes the difference between busy-ness and productivity.

For example, we created **The "Body Signals" Program**—a subluxation-based, patient education and marketing system. It's a great way to "get in the conversation" that is already happening all around you. Each month, we focus on one symptom or "Body Signal," as our condition of the month. This is the central topic for all content coming out of our practice that month—our articles of the week, research, testimonials, success stories, and social media content. All promotional activity builds toward an end-of-month workshop, webinar, and more.

See an example of a Marketing Calendar and check out this free video on creating your Marketing Calendar here: theremarkablepractice. com/Attraction.

The Body Signals Program is powerful in that it allows us to have the **Cause and Effect** conversation with patients about symptoms and conditions. It empowers you to be relevant in the marketplace—you can "speak into people's listening." People are actively looking for help for specific issues. Now they can find you.

The term Body Signals is informative on its own—and tends to *"start the conversation"* that we want to be having. It empowers our patients to speak to their friends and families confidently. And it is also a great way to get your Team focused on what we are promoting every month. We've met over ten thousand New Patients through this program over the years—and the many DCs that use this system around the world have attracted and helped many thousands more.

Point is: we use these patient-education frameworks as marketing tools to get our practice in the conversation. We plug it all into our calendar, and everyone knows exactly how it's going to unfold. You can do the same.

Then, we also leverage social media to promote the content, to post and share our articles. The marketing we do around our Body Signals

Program is not only internal. We also go out into the community and do corporate talks on the subject, and of course it serves as the framework for our web-based and social media campaigns, as well.

The Body Signals Program is now filling clinics around the world with motivated New Patients looking for help. Learn more about the Body Signals Program here: theremarkablepractice.com/tbr-bodysignals.

Now that you have a plan and a calendar, you're poised and positioned to go out into the marketplace. It feels good, doesn't it, to actually have a strategy for new business development? It's a hell of a lot better than winging it, right? Instead of being in constant reactive mode—saying, "Oh Man, we need more new patients, let's throw something together and do some marketing"—now you have a real plan in place.

Instead of just making it all up last minute as you go and cobbling together some kind of stressful, unproductive patient marketing effort, now everybody on the team knows in advance exactly how things are going to unfold. They know: *here's our twelve-month marketing calendar, here's what we're going to do, follow this system, this program.*

At last, you have a system.

As I mentioned in the beginning of this chapter, effective marketing comes down to three things: Mindset, Strategy and Tactics.

Of course, having a great system in place for attracting new patients still means nothing if you can't close the deal, i.e., *convert* that prospective new patient to an active one. We are not in the business of marketing chiropractic—or doing Day One's and Day Two's—we are in the business of saving lives on the table.

I like to say, "We can only help the ones we convert." It's a linear progression, just like any other relationship: first you're on the dance floor, then you're dating each other, then you're engaged, and then you're married.

> *We can only help the ones that we Convert.*

So how do you take someone from a Perspective New Patient to a Converted Active Patient? How do you bridge the gap from Attracting New Patients to Converting them? Now that you're in the conversation, now that people are reaching out to you for help, how do you take that prospect and turn them into an Ideal Active "Practice Member?"

In the next chapter we will do a deep dive on the most critical part of your Patient Process—The Conversion Process—and you'll discover how to **turn a prospective new patient from a "skeptic" into a "believer."**

## SUMMARY

- Attraction Systems refer to your systems for Marketing and Promotions.
- There are three sources of Prospective New Patients: internal, external and digital.
- Your Marketing Plan should encompass all three tributaries to the river of New Patients.
- Capture your marketing plan in a marketing calendar that is visible to your team.
- Your Attraction is a Reflection of Your Certainty.
- Your Market Message must be relevant to your target demographic.
- You must get in the conversation that your Ideal Prospects are already having.

*To Download All the Chapter Resources, Go Here:*
1. theremarkablepractice.com/Attraction

*To Learn More, Check Out These Remarkable Resources*
2. Body Signals Program: theremarkablepractice.com/tbr-bodysignals
3. TRP Academy: theremarkablepractice.com/tbr-academy
4. TRP DC and CA Process and Procedure Manuals: theremarkablepractice.com/tbr-manuals
5. TRP Private Coaching: theremarkablepractice.com/tbr-coaching
6. Remarkable Live Immersion Events: theremarkablepractice.com/tbr-events

1     2     3

4     5     6

# CHAPTER FIVE

# SYSTEMS OF CONVERSION

*"People do not care how much you know—*
*until they know how much you care."*

—*Unknown*

What do we mean when we talk about Patient Conversion? For my Team, our goal has always been to create what we call **"True Conversion,"** which is part of our sequential approach to creating the ideal patients who make up a truly remarkable practice.

In other words, for us conversion is part of a continuum. We attract people, we convert them, and we retain them. We're not just focused on getting patients started. We convert them with the intention to retain them and get them under regular chiropractic care for life. That's our objective: **we want people to adopt chiropractic as a lifestyle success strategy for healthy human beings,** and not just a short-term treatment modality for a crisis or symptom.

Sounds pretty good, doesn't it? But it took me awhile until I really *got* it and realized what true conversion is all about. Even though philosophically I was aligned with this concept, in practice I had a blind spot. I would get people started on their chiropractic care without first creating clarity and alignment around their goals.

I didn't take the time to get to know them and understand their immediate, short-term and long-term goals with their health. I didn't take time to help them really learn what was available to them through chiropractic.

Why did I behave like that? I was operating with an assumption that these patients were going to get great results anyway, and that's what mattered. They were going to be happy because we were taking great care of them. Yes, I knew it was important that they learned, as well, but I trusted that they'd be available for that as the care continued. As long as they were getting great results, it was only logical that they would stay under our care.

I was wrong.

That's just not how people operate. At the end of the day, most of us have been brought up under a medical model. We go see a doctor when we're in crisis, when we have a symptom. The doctor gives us a pill to make us feel better, and then we don't need the doctor anymore. At least until the next time we're sick or there's a problem.

That's the allopathic model, and of course, as purpose-driven chiropractors, it's the kind of thinking we're trying to overcome. Why do we feel that way? Because we know that crisis management or symptom management is not going to produce the kind of enduring health and happiness that we all want.

As chiropractors, we certainly do help people who are in crisis and already symptomatic—and we're very good at that. We welcome them with open arms. But most of us really want to do more for our people. We want to do more than just bring them from "sick to not sick." We want to inspire them to go even further on the health spectrum—from "not sick" to "healthy" and then help them stay there, through Chiropractic Care.

That's what makes our profession unique. That's what makes the Wellness Paradigm distinct. But getting your patients to embrace this requires **True Conversion**, not just closing people and getting them to "start care." It's not just about "getting people checked" or having them dabble in Chiropractic. It's about showing people that Chiropractic is a Lifestyle Success Strategy for healthy human beings. It is about Attracting, Converting and ultimately, creating and Retaining Ideal Patients. I believe that it is all about **Retention**.

We do our best work and get the best results when patients follow our recommendations and stay under care. They get the best clinical outcomes, our practice grows, and we enjoy the most fulfillment. Everybody wins. But more on that in the next chapter.

Here's what I know:

## Retention Begins at Conversion.

Steven Covey taught us to *"begin with the end in mind."* We must take this approach when designing and executing our Conversion Process. If we want people to stay under care—beyond initial crisis care—then we will need to be highly deliberate about that outcome from the beginning. Staying under care is not the natural default—but people will continue getting adjusted regularly (like you and I) *if* they *want* to...*if* they understand *why* they should. That is what this chapter is about: **Turning Believers into Understanders.**

The True Conversion Process starts and ends with our original Conversion Premise:

> ### *Conversion is a reflection of your conviction.*

That means *owning* your recommendations for care, as a doctor and an expert—knowing what's best for the patient, understanding it, and believing it to your core.

There is a Latin expression in property law: *Nemo Dat*, which means you can't sell what you don't own. It may seem obvious and straightforward that you should believe what you say. You should tell patients exactly what they need to do to get what they want. Nothing more. Nothing less. As my friend and colleague, Dr. Pete Camiolo likes to say, "Tell them the truth, the whole truth and nothing but the truth..."

I am sure that we can all agree that telling someone that they need more care than they actually need is out of integrity. Right? Well, I will suggest that telling someone that they need *less* care than they actually need is also out of integrity.

But the truth of the matter is that many—perhaps most—chiropractors will tell their patients that they need less care than they actually do. Why do we do that? It's because we're afraid to tell our patients how bad it really is, and what they really need to do to get the results they seek. We're unsure that the patient will *go for it*, so we minimize the severity of the problem and our recommendations for care.

This is out of integrity.

> *Stop reading people and start leading people.*

If you want to help more people, then you are going to have to convert more people to the care that they actually need. In order to succeed in Conversion, you have to start being real with people. Most people have a really good B.S. Meter. It's innate. If you're full of it, everybody is going to pick up on it. The only way to show real conviction is to tell your patients the truth, the whole truth, and nothing but the truth.

## START WITH THE END IN MIND

You must keep your eye on the goal. As chiropractors, our goal is to get as many people as possible—as many families as possible—into the end zone: **Wellness Care** (or at least, **Maintenance Care**).

To do that, we must "start with the end in mind" and that begins with the Conversion Process. You can't do what I once tried to do, which was to get them started for one reason and then try to flip them to stay for another reason once they start.

You must meet them where they are. That's where I got it wrong. Philosophically, I was so far on the wellness side of the fence that I forgot there even was a fence. I had the curse of knowledge, and it made me blind to how I needed to communicate to a layperson. I was so committed to challenging the medical paradigm and changing the patient's paradigm; meanwhile, my patients didn't even know what a paradigm was. I was irrelevant.

> *I was so far on the wellness side of the fence*
> *that I forgot there even was a fence.*

Whenever I started working with a new patient, I would deliver the "adjustment," teach them about subluxation, and I'd explain their problem: *"There's a spinal joint that's out of healthy alignment and not moving properly. It's causing inflammation and nerve pressure—which is resulting in stress in the nervous system and interference to the expression of your innate intelligence, and in your case, it's causing discomfort."*

They seemed to get it. And they started care (they let me adjust them).

All in all, I *thought* I converted them. I showed them what their problem was and even showed them the root cause of their problem. Then I explained how I would be able to correct the problem, and proceeded to follow through with my promise.

Sounds pretty good, right? Not so fast. What do you think I got in return? "You're wonderful, you're awesome, chiropractic works. I feel better. I'm out of here. I'll come back the next time I have a problem."

Huh? Time and again, I found myself scratching my head and wondering: *what happened here? We got great results. Didn't you listen to me when I told you that you needed to get under regular chiropractic care?*

Have you ever been there?

Looking back, I realized I didn't do a good job in the very beginning with several critical steps. These critical steps (which we are going to cover in detail) would have changed everything for me had I known them.

From a high level, my first misstep was that I did not make sure that they felt heard—that I understood what brought them to the office in the first place. I did not make sure that they really owned their problem (and it's probably not what you're thinking right now—more on that shortly). I did not establish good goals for their care. We did not have clear and shared objectives. And then I did a poor job at setting good "Expectations and Agreements"—specifically around their Care Plan.

Even more specifically, I did not do a good job at **pre-framing**. I didn't set the patient's expectations for what was to come—for the short term, midterm and long term. I wasn't explaining the arc of care—and the benefits of each.

When patients lack **Clarity** from the beginning—Patient Retention is doomed. This is why it is critical to understand that **Retention begins at Conversion.** You must establish clarity for the patient as to what their problem is, what's possible for them as far as correction, and what needs to happen for them to reach their goals. Eventually, I mastered this communication and summarized it in the infographic below. This simple but powerful image illustrates the three legs of the patient journey back to Wellness: starting with Initial Intensive Care, then Corrective Care, and then Wellness or Maintenance Care.

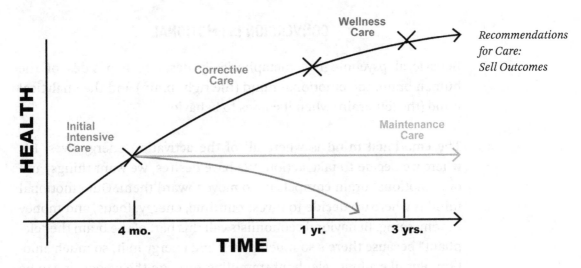

The objective of Initial Intensive Care is to stop the damage, stabilize the problem, so that they can start the healing process. Then, they are promoted to the next stage, Corrective Care, which is all about strengthening the body so that they can do the things they want to do without experiencing a relapse or setback every time they try to use their body. Finally, they can graduate to Wellness Care—the ongoing, regular care for patients whose goal is to keep getting healthier and stronger over time. For others, specifically those who are satisfied with where they are after their initial care, and simply want to protect their new level of health and not slide backwards, we recommend and provide scheduled "Maintenance Care."

This three-stage framework to patient care works extremely well. But only if you set expectations of how it's all going to go from the beginning. That's where I went wrong.

But we're putting the cart before the horse a little. Let's double back and do a deep dive on the Conversion Process; specifically, let's discuss the **emotional element of conversion**.

## CONVERSION IS EMOTIONAL

Behavioral psychologists metaphorically describe two sides of the human brain: the emotional mind (the right brain) and the analytical mind (the left brain) when it comes to behavior.

The **emotional mind** is where all of the activation energy lives. It's where we decide to take action. We have desires, we want things, and our emotional brain compels us to move toward them. Our emotional mind is where we decide to invest our time, energy, focus, and money in something. Behavioral economists call this part of the brain the "elephant" because there's so much power and energy in it, so much emotion. But like a huge elephant trampling through the woods, it can be wild and clumsy.

Which is where the **analytical mind** comes in. Like a tiny rider sitting on top of the powerful elephant—the analytical mind tries to steer the animal through the jungle, keeping him on the path. The rider is the analyst—he wants information, directions, data...

If you think about the elephant as a kind of gas pedal—always wanting to accelerate, to act now, to take action—then the man on top is the brake. The two are constantly competing with each other. The emotional mind wants to move where the analytic mind wants to hold back and gather more information.

How does this all tie into conversion?

### *Conversion is Emotional. Retention is Intellectual.*

**Conversion is emotional.** People convert based on *what they feel.*

I used to screw this up royally. What I didn't realize when I was starting out was that people begin chiropractic care based on what they *feel* when they're in your practice in those first two days. Do they feel like, *"I'm in the right place"*...or, "I have found my doctor?" Do they feel like they are where they are supposed to be, and they have found their solution...they have found the person who's going to *help them get what they want*?

You have to realize: that's *why* they are there. It's why they start care. Not because of what they understand, but because of how you make them feel. Later on, this will change. People will *start* care because of what they *feel*. But they will *stay* under care because of what *they know*. They will stay because of what they have learned and now understand about chiropractic. (More on that in the next chapter on Retention.) But first, we must get them to start.

When a New Patient commits to care (The Conversion Process), they are a "Believer," but they don't yet *understand* anything. They don't understand the body, the spine, the nervous system. They don't understand subluxation or the adjustment or the Innate Intelligence of the body. They don't understand the Wellness Paradigm or the Chiropractic Principle. They don't *understand* anything. They *believe* you.

They're a **Believer**.

Unfortunately, all too often what happens is that doctors struggle to convert New Patients because they are trying to teach them everything that they never wanted to know about Chiropractic. They want to give them tons of data and information about chiropractic. Too many DCs think that if they give the prospective New Patient plenty of information, they will of course make the logical decision to begin care. Unfortunately, this informational approach **engages the analytical mind** and the brake gets pulled. The brain stops and says, *"Wait a minute, this sounds important, I need to pause and go home and get more information—I'll ask Dr. Google what he thinks."* And we know where it goes from there.

Everything just freezes. Conversion is halted in its tracks.

Now, ask yourself this: what would happen instead if we held back from delivering all that information and just made sure we **stay focused on the person and their story**? Why are they here? What do they think their problem is? How is it affecting their life? What are they trying to get accomplished? What are their goals?

Remember: **Conversion is Emotional**.

(Retention, on the other hand, is intellectual. People will stay under care based on what they know, as we'll see in the next chapter.)

## THE LIFE EFFECT

We call this "**The Life Effect**" because it's all the stuff they want to do, or *have* to do, but are no longer capable of. They want to work out, run, surf, ski, do CrossFit. They want to be able to pick up their grandkids. In some cases, it's not an option to not do certain things, and so they have no choice but to persevere through the pain. There are things they *have* to do, like hang Sheetrock, or lay bricks, or sit at a computer for their work.

Point is: we need to listen to *them* more. What are they trying to accomplish? What is their objective? What are they trying to get done? What are their immediate and short-term goals? What are their long-term goals?

> *Each patient has a story, and it's your job*
> *to get them to tell you that story.*

They've given you their reference points on a GPS system. Point A is where they are today. Points X, Y, and Z are where they want to go. X is their intermediate goal, Y is their short-term goal, and Z is their long-term goal.

If you want to achieve true conversion, you have to connect with that voice in their emotional brain that's crying out, "Can you get me there? Are you the expert I need to see?" You must show them that you've listened, that you understand them and why they're here. You've heard how it's affected their life, and what they are trying to achieve.

If you can successfully convey all of that to the patient, that's called making **an empathetic connection**.

An empathetic connection is what triggers the brain to become available. The patient opens up and thinks to themselves, *Hey, you know what? I like this doctor, she listens to me, she gets me, she gets my story.*

Having made sure the patient stays in their heart and not their head, having successfully kept them *in their story*—in the emotional part of what brought them to your office—you have now created that connection.

By helping them stay in their heart emotionally, you've made them a believer.

Every new patient who comes into your office only wants two things: **Connection and Direction**.

And importantly, they are looking for Connection *first* and, then, Direction. If you get the first part right—if you make that empathetic connection properly—they'll be *more than* open to your direction. They'll listen to everything you say through a different lens. Your direction will sound to them now like *solving*, and they will love you for it.

> *Every patient only wants two things: Connection and Direction.*

When you successfully establish an empathetic connection with a patient, they will *want* to hear your recommendations for care. They'll want to move forward. Why? Because in their mind, you understand them now. Earlier, their brain would have recoiled from information. But now, they are **available** and ready and eager to hear your direction.

The education piece will come next, in the chapter about Retention. But first let's walk through the various steps you need to know to create your own conversion system.

## ATTRACT TO CONVERT, CONVERT TO RETAIN

If you're like a lot of chiropractors I encounter, you may *think* you're doing the right thing when it comes to conversion. You *are* trying to pre-frame. But in reality, you're giving them too much information too early on. Your heart is in the right place; you've got the right intentions. But there's still a lack of awareness. You're not fully taking in the fact that there remains a huge gulf between you and your patient. You're like I used to be: so far on the other side of the fence that you forget your patient doesn't even know there is a fence.

It can become a real handicap in communications, which is why again I encourage doctors to **slow down to speed up**.

Make the empathetic connection with the patient and do it for *their* sake not yours. You don't need it. But they do. There is already a disconnect with the person sitting in front of you. Your goal is to make it smaller not wider.

So how do you go about making this connection in a systematic way?

I did it gradually by learning from my mistakes. As readers know by now, I used to suck at conversion. I was horrible at it because by nature

I'm a solver. I don't even need to hear the end of your sentence; I already know what you're going to say. I'm a very fast processor *and* I'm impatient, which is admittedly a terrible combination.

So when I met with patients, I would rush them. My attitude was: *yep, I know exactly what's going on. Good. I've got enough. Let's go, let's move, let's fix this, let's solve.*

Then, when I saw how badly my approach was working, I knew I had to make a change. Conversion became a learned skill for me. First, I had to identify a very specific set of provocative questions that would get them to open up to me, not just listen to me yapping at them.

> *I knew I had to stop* telling *them and start* asking *them.*

I created a system for getting them to reveal themselves, again a kind of unearthing or inside-out experience. I learned how to ask the right questions, ones that would provoke revealing and insightful responses. To see some of my favorite provocative questions to ask, go here and download "The 33 Most Critical Questions to Ask a New Patient": theremarkablepractice.com/Conversion.

## THE FOUR AGREEMENTS

Behavioral psychology teaches us that, when it comes to *how* people decide to take action, there are four distinct steps. I am going to share this formula with you now, but only if you promise to use it for good! I'm not kidding...**this is a superpower**. What I am about to teach you *changes careers*. I've literally seen people triple their practices using the insights they learned from my Four Agreements Formula.

Why is this so powerful? It comes down to fundamental behavioral economics and *how* human beings make the decisions they do—specifically around how they invest their time, energy, focus, and money. When you understand this, you can leverage communication technology *on their behalf* to help them convert.

Make sense? OK, so here's how it goes: when you want someone to take action, you have to follow these four steps. First, they must agree on the **Problem (The Life Effect)**. Second, they must agree on the **Goal (The Objectives)**. Third, they then must agree on the **Path (The Recommendations for Care)**. And fourth, they must agree on the **Plan (The Financial Agreement)**.

*The Four Agreements*

> ***The Four Agreements:***
> ***Agree on the Problem,***
> ***Agree on the Goal,***
> ***Agree on the Path,***
> ***Agree on the Plan.***

These are the Four Agreements. They are critical in the Conversion Process. So much so—you cannot leave them to chance. You must systematize this process and create automaticity in it. Every patient must experience this process. We call it **"The Story Cycle."**

THE FOUR AGREEMENTS
A Conversion Formula

· Agreements, not steps. · Do not skip over agreements. · Do in this order.

#1 AGREE ON THE PROBLEM — Symptom vs. Cause vs. Life Effect

#2 AGREE ON THE GOAL — Immediate, Short-Term, & Long-Term Objectives

#3 AGREE ON THE PATH — Rec's for Care

#4 AGREE ON THE PLAN — The Financial Arrangement

the REMARKABLE practice
theremarkablepractice.com

## THE STORY CYCLE

If you look at this like a baseball diamond—Home plate is at the top—this is where the Perspective New Patient walks in your front door. Imagine they're coming in carrying something in their hands: their story. It's their prized possession, their belief system, the sum of their experiences. It's everything they've been told by their parents, siblings, friends, teachers, doctors, insurance companies, television, and more.

It's their story, and it can be a scary one. Your first step, therefore, is to make an empathetic connection with them. So First Base is when you *get* their story. You do that by asking them a very specific series of questions: What do they think their problem is? How is this effecting their life? And what are their goals? You listen and make the patient feel like they've been heard. That you understand them. You must get their story.

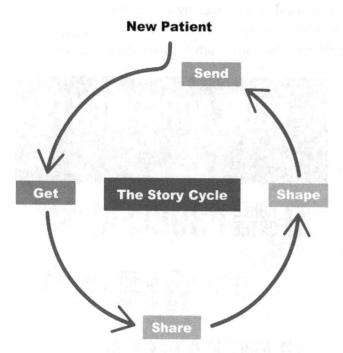

*The Story Cycle*

Now that they've become available to you, you can move on to the next stage in the cycle. Second Base is when you **share** *your* story, the chiropractic story. At this point, the patient is ready to hear it—they are available. They literally hear the words differently than they would have before. It resonates. It makes sense to them. You give them your best recommendations, and the recommendations are well received. The patient is compelled to take action. They convert.

Having heard your story, they are now primed to engage and move forward. You start challenging their belief system and teaching them a new paradigm, a new way to look at life and health and their body. A world of new possibilities opens up to them. They start getting adjusted, clearing their nervous system, and they start healing.

All in all, they are now processing things differently and getting their health back. They are thinking differently. They're exercising, eating right, sleeping better. Everything's falling into place. You shape their new story, which means you're now at Third Base on the Story Cycle.

As you continue to shape the story, they start telling a different story than the one they came in with. You **send** them back into the world to share this new story. They head for Home Base. Chiropractic is now part of their ongoing story. Not only that but *you*, doctor, are part of the story, which leads to referrals and sets the process in motion all over again.

So that's the Story Cycle. It's just four steps: **Get, Share, Shape, Send.**

Of course, where I used to get it wrong was that I'd leapfrog straight from Home Base to Second Base. I'd skip right over the "getting their story" part because I thought I didn't need to know it. I was a principled, educated chiropractor with lots of experience and a strong philosophy. I didn't know the patient's goals or what they thought their problem was. I didn't know their trauma history, what they were allergic to, what supplements they were taking. I didn't think I needed all that stuff. All I needed was my X-ray, my hands, my scope, and I could do what needed to be done.

As it turned out, leapfrogging over making that empathetic connection and jumping right into recommendations for care—jumping ahead to solving and direction—created a huge disconnect for people coming into the office looking for help. I suspect my recommendations for care felt like *selling* to my patients. How could it not? In their eyes, how could I possibly have a solution for them without having asked them any questions or tried to understand their problem?

I shudder to think how many people I blew it with—all because I didn't slow down to make that connection. If I knew then what I know now, I would have realized that when you slow down in the beginning, everything speeds up later, after you've made that empathetic connection.

But if you mess up like I did, and like so many chiropractors do, you get the opposite. The conversion screeches to a stop because you went too fast on the front end. The one misstep creates a real tug of war, a power struggle, because the patient has questions and is now confused.

*Confusion Never Converts.*

If you do it right, however, if you follow the Story Cycle and the process for conversion, you will see success like never before. Getting conversion right is perhaps the most life-changing part of your journey. Which is why it's so important to take your time and adhere to the exact sequence of this system I've created.

## THE TRUE CONVERSION PROCESS

The Conversion Process is a four-day process, and it aligns with the Four Agreements.

**Day one** is about *connection and discovery*, doing the consultation, asking the questions, doing the examination.

**Day two** is about *ownership*: the patient taking ownership of their problem, their goals, and their path. It's when the real commitment happens. The person says yes to their care plan and to the financial arrangement.

**Day three**, then, is about setting *expectations and agreements* and patient training.

**Day four** is the *paradigm shift and equipping* the patient to get great results.

It is on that fourth day that true conversion is completed. The patient walks out as an "**Understander**."

Why? Because you converted them in their story (emotional mind)—*and now spoke to and satisfied their analytical mind*.

You took them from **Skeptic** to **Believer**, and now you will take them from **Believer** to **Understander**. Now the journey has begun. They are well on their way to becoming an Ideal Patient. This is the threshold where we go from Conversion to Retention.

In the following chapter, you will learn how to *retain* patients—and get them to stay under regular chiropractic care—by creating **Understanders**. People who understand chiropractic, want chiropractic. They stay under regular care, get our best work and get the best results. Like the old saying goes: *they stay, pay and refer*. They are Ideal Patients. And a true business does not leave that to chance. A true business has a system that predictably creates this outcome, in fact, it makes this transformation nearly automatic.

## SUMMARY

- Ideal Patients "Stay, Pay and Refer"—this happens when they start strong. This requires True Conversion.
- The True Conversion Process is essentially one communication that happens over a four-day period.
- Conversion is Emotional (people start care based on what they feel). Retention is intellectual (people stay under care based on what they *know*).
- Day One is about Connection and Discovery—make an empathetic connection so that the Perspective New Patient (PNP) feels heard. Then they will be ready to receive your

best recommendations for care. Discovery describes your NP Consultation and Examination.

- Day Two is about the PNP taking ownership of the Four Agreements: Agree on the Problem (the Life Effect), Agree on the Goals (immediate, short-term and long-term goals), Agree on the Path (Recommendations) and Agree on the Plan (the financial agreement).
- Day Three is about Expectations and Agreements—reviewing office policies and patient training. Teach practice members how to be ideal patients.
- Day Four is about creating a Paradigm Shift and equipping a patient to get the best results (The New Patient Orientation).
- The True Conversion Process takes a PNP from **Skeptic** to **Believer**.

*To Download All the Chapter Resources, Go Here:*
1. theremarkablepractice.com/Conversion

*To Learn More, Check Out These Remarkable Resources*
2. TRP Academy: theremarkablepractice.com/tbr-academy
3. TRP DC and CA Process and Procedure Manuals: theremarkablepractice.com/tbr-manuals
4. TRP Private Coaching: theremarkablepractice.com/tbr-coaching
5. Remarkable Live Immersion Events: theremarkablepractice. com/tbr-events

*1*  *2*  *3*  *4*  *5*

## CHAPTER SIX

# SYSTEMS OF RETENTION

*"Begin with the end in mind."*
—Stephen Covey

If Attraction is a reflection of your Certainty and Conversion is a Reflection of your Conviction, then **Retention is a reflection of your Clarity**.

Your Patient Retention, usually measured in the metric Patient Visit Average (or PVA—the average number of visits that a patient receives over their lifetime) is a reflection of your clarity, your Team's clarity— and the patient's clarity.

What do we mean by clarity in this context? The patient must have clarity around *why they should stay under regular chiropractic care—why they* should be investing their time, energy, focus, and money in it. They must be clear around the value of continuing regular chiropractic care.

I can't stress enough how important this is. Patients do not usually drop out of care because they are disappointed. They don't leave because they no longer feel that you are helping them—or that you've upset them in some way. No, patients leave because they lose **clarity** around why they should stay.

This may sound obvious, but it's so very true. As a practitioner and business owner, it's up to you to make sure the patient understands not only why they should *start* care but also why they should stay under care. You can never, ever take that for granted.

> *Patients leave because they lose clarity*
> *around why they should stay.*

Think of it from the patient's perspective. Glimpse inside their mind for a moment. In the previous chapter, we learned about the left brain and the right brain, the emotional mind, and the analytical mind. You must realize that humans are economists—they are constantly weighing the value of continued chiropractic care. Think about it, they have

 to continue to invest their time, energy, and focus to get what they want—and there is a lot competing for those resources.

It's like a **scale that they're constantly trying to balance**. As soon as the scale tips—and the time, energy, focus, and money become *heavier* than the value of continued chiropractic care, they're gone.

Which is why *you* must be constantly creating **clarity** around the value of continued care. If you don't, you'll see more and more patients slipping out the side door.

And we all know how much that sucks.

I've been there. You've been there. You know how it goes: one moment everything's great, the patient is improving, and then you get the *Dear John* letter. "Dear Doc, I love everything you stand for, and I've really had a great experience, but I'm going to take a break for a while and see how it goes..."

Man, those notes are the worst. I would rather be punched in the face. Look, we are all disappointed when someone does not start care—but I *hate* it when they drop out of care. When this happens, I feel like we've really blown it for them somehow. One day they were part of the Tribe—part of the family—and the next day, they are gone. I used to think that this would bother me less as my practice grew or I got more years under my belt—but I was wrong. It never gets easier when people drop out of care.

Because this bothered me so much—and I realized all the best results happen when people stay under care, I had to figure this out. Why do people drop out of care? And more importantly, why do people stay? I wanted to become a master of Patient Retention—and I did.

## REPLATIENTS

Too many chiropractors find themselves desperately searching for more New Patients every month. I'd love to say that it was "Mission Driven," but all too often they're in a panic because their existing patients are dropping out of care left and right. Why the attrition?

I certainly understand this panic. I used to experience it myself, until I figured out what I am going to share with you now. The key to keeping patients—and I mean for the long term—is that you've got to create "**Understanders.**" In fact, you've got to turn Skeptics into Believers—and then turn Believers into Understanders. This transformation begins during the Conversion Process and defines the **Retention Process**.

Marketing and promoting to bring in New Patients is indeed critical in creating your Remarkable Practice as Part of Your Remarkable Life. But like Dr. Demartini says: wanting to attract more New Patients should be "based on inspiration—not desperation." New Patient Attraction should be purpose-driven, with the goal of helping more people and expanding your reach—not survival-driven; desperately looking for *"Replatients"* to substitute for the ones that drop out because you didn't manage them well in the first place.

Having come this far in the book, you're probably starting to realize that when all is said and done, the real secret to growing a world-class practice is *not just* finding New Patients but rather *keeping* the great patients that are already in your office.

If you can keep the people you're already taking care of—if you can *retain* them—you will experience the powerful compound effect of collecting Ideal Patients. When you create Ideal Patients—and collect Ideal Patients—you get to do your best work, get the best results, and your practice grows. Everybody wins.

Look, I'm not here to tell you what success looks like for you. For that, you must return to *your* Vision Story and *your* Core Values. But I can tell you that for *me*, and for a lot of successful chiropractors that I work with, **Retention is critically important**. Yes, it's good for business, but if you are like me, you know that people do best when they follow your recommendations and stay under regular care for life.

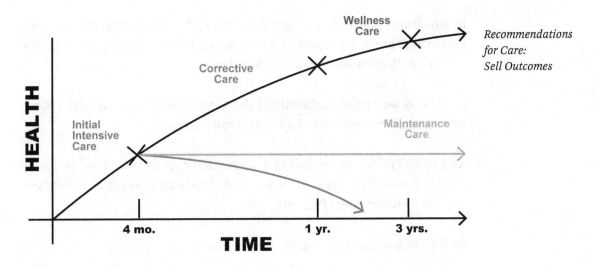

Consider the Patient Lifecycle as three legs of a journey: they start with **Initial Intensive Care**, then graduate to **Corrective Care**, and then they move into **Wellness Care**.

The objective of *Initial Intensive Care* is to stabilize the problems and stop the damage. Next it's onto *Corrective Care* where the goal is to strengthen the body so that the patient can get back to doing the things that they want to do and have to do. Then finally, they graduate to *Wellness Care*. The objective of Wellness Care is to stay subluxation-free and continue their health and healing trajectory over a lifetime. In our practice, the goal has always been get everybody into the "end zone" of Wellness Care for life. This is what we call *"Lifetime Family Wellness."* And every step of the process must be consistent with that—from Day One.

This is a huge part of *my* Vision Story. My vision for success is to create a place where families can find a better way to better health—where they cannot only receive the chiropractic care that they need but also get an education that will change their way of thinking—and their behavior—for life. I want them to be equipped and supported for the kind of lifestyle that's going to lead to the best possible outcomes for them over their entire lifetime. I want multiple generations of family members in my office: coming in to get checked and getting chiropractic care regularly. That is my vision of success, and it has everything to do with retention. What's your Vision of Success?

Go to this web page to download the Core Values Exercise and Vision Story Exercise: *theremarkablepractice.com/retention*.

As I said, Patient Retention is a huge factor in my vision of success: attract prospective Ideal Patients, convert them into Ideal Patients—and then **collect** Ideal Patients.

So let's talk about creating Ideal Patients.

Let's revisit the concept of the **Believer** vs. the **Understander**.

## COLLECTING HELIUM BALLOONS

When a patient commits to care initially, they are a **Believer**. They *believe* you. They believe that you will help them get what they want. They believe that they are in the right place. But they do not *understand* anything. They do not understand chiropractic. They do not understand subluxation—or the adjustment. They do not understand how their body really works—or how it really heals. They do not understand the spine or the nervous system for that matter. They do not understand the Chiropractic Principle or the Wellness Paradigm. They don't *understand* anything. They believe you.

Believers are great, but they are "heavy." They have lots of questions and even objections and pushback. They want to do a consultation on every visit. Of course they do—they're learning an entirely new and different way to look at health and healing. That is exactly how it *should* be at this point. They are a Believer, and you've got to carry them on your back. And they are heavy.

But here's the thing: you do not have to *believe* in Chiropractic—you can *understand* Chiropractic. And once you understand Chiropractic, you want Chiropractic. Like you and I—we understand Chiropractic. We are **Understanders**.

You want to convert every patient into an Understander. Understanders are weightless.

Consider the Understander, the person who really understands chiropractic. People like your family and my family. These people want to come in, get checked, and get adjusted. "Check me. Adjust me. Power's on! See you next week..." and they're out the door.

Believers are heavy to carry around. Understanders are "weightless." You can gather them up and collect them like helium balloons. Which means you can handle more of them. You can serve more patients, have a bigger impact, and make a better living.

### *The Key to Patient Retention: Convert Believers into Understanders.*

The key to Patient Retention is to turn Believers into Understanders. Understanders follow the doctor's recommendations, get the best results, stay under care, and refer others. It's a total Win-Win-Win. It's what we all want. Strong Patient Retention creates stability and predictable growth. It creates scalability and durability, and it's one of the most integral parts of this journey to creating a Remarkable Practice as Part of a Remarkable Life.

# THE DIRTY DOZEN

"Okay, Dr. Franson," you're probably saying. "I get that we want to turn Believers into Understanders, and I get that once people understand Chiropractic, they want Chiropractic. But what exactly do they need to understand?"

I get this question all the time, and it's a great one. To help people with this, I put together what I call the **Dirty Dozen**—the twelve things every patient needs to know to be healthy. (Otherwise known as the "twelve things that everyone needs to know, and they'll never leave you.")

I curated this list of concepts over the more than twenty years I spent taking care of patients at the highest level—seeing hundreds of patients a day—over 1,000 patient visits a week. I consider these "concepts" that people need in order to understand the value of regular, lifetime Chiropractic Care. These are the essence of retention. I speak from deep expertise on this subject—our practice enjoyed a PVA of over 300 for over fifteen years. That means that the average patient that started care with us stayed over 300 visits.

I'll suggest that if you can get patients to understand these twelve things, they will never leave you.

1. **Healthy Is Normal.** Sick is abnormal. You're *supposed* to be healthy. You're designed to be healthy. Being unhealthy is abnormal. Even though "sick" has become the norm, it's still abnormal.

2. **Your Body Is Intelligent.** Your body is smart. It's not stupid, so stop treating it like it is. When you have symptoms, conditions, crisis...when you experience "Body Signals"...when your innately intelligent body is talking to you, don't stifle that communication with drugs and chemicals. You must listen to

# 12 THINGS YOU NEED TO KNOW TO BE HEALTHY

**YOU ARE DESIGNED TO BE HEALTHY**
**1**
Healthy is Normal. Unhealthy is Abnormal.

**YOUR BODY IS SMART**
**2**
There is an Innate Intelligence that runs your body.

**INNATE INTELLIGENCE COMMUNICATES ACROSS THE NERVOUS SYSTEM**
**3**
The Nervous System helps us adapt to and deal with STRESS.

**YOUR SPINE IS YOUR SUIT OF ARMOR**
**4**
Your Spine protects your nerve system spinal cord – like skull protects brain.

**STRESS CAUSES A CONDITION KNOWN AS SUBLUXATION**
**5**
Subluxations Create Interference in the Nervous System Communications.

**SUBLUXATION CAUSES DYSFUNCTION THAT CAN MANIFEST AS SYMPTOMS AND CONDITIONS**
**6**
Subluxations are the root cause of many common health issues.

**YOUR LIFE IS UNNATURALLY STRESSFUL**
**7**
Modern Life is unnaturally fast-paced and filled with stress.

**SUBLUXATION IS CAUSED BY STRESS**
**8**
3 Types of Stress that cause Subluxation are Thoughts, Toxins and Traumas.

**HOW WOULD YOU KNOW IF YOU HAVE SUBLUXATION?**
**9**
Only a Chiropractor is trained to objectively test for Subluxation.

**WHAT SHOULD YOU DO IF YOU HAVE SUBLUXATION?**
**10**
Only Specific Chiropractic Adjustments correct Subluxation.

**WE ARE ON A MISSION TO HELP OUR COMMUNITY**
**11**
Everyone who wishes to be healthy must be checked by a Chiropractor.

**I NEED YOUR HELP**
**12**
If You Do Not Tell Your Family and Friends – Who Will?

the
**REMARKABLE !**
practice
www.theremarkablepractice.com

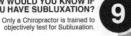

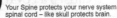

your body. It is a self-regulating, self-healing organism. Your body is smart.

3. **Innate Intelligence Courses across the Nervous System.** Your nervous system is the Master System of your body. It's the intelligence network—the communication system.

4. **Your Spine Is Your Suit of Armor.** It protects your spinal cord. Your skull is the helmet that protects your brain. Your spine is the suit of armor that protects your spinal cord.

5. **Life Is Stressful.** Modern life is unnaturally stressful, and stress causes a condition called subluxation.

6. **What Is Subluxation?** Subluxation creates interference in the communication between the body and the brain. Misalignment and/or dysfunction in the spinal joints creates stress on the nervous system and alters normal brain function, interfering with the body's ability to regulate and heal itself.

7. **What Does Subluxation Cause in the Body?** Subluxation creates stress on the nervous system and alters brain function. This may result in a stress response and adaptive physiology which can result in common health conditions if not corrected.

8. **What Causes *Your* Subluxation Specifically?** Patients need to know what causes their subluxations in the first place—and what may cause them to return and become subluxation patterns. They need to understand the three T's that cause subluxation: Thoughts, Toxins, and Traumas. They should know that subluxation can be caused by the obvious things like car accidents, sports injuries, and slips and falls. But even more commonly by poor posture, sleep positions, and conditions in the workplace. In the modern world, tech stress is a very real

health issue. People spend too much time sitting in front of a screen—computers, tablets, and mobile phones. If sitting is the new smoking, then screens are the new crack.

9. **How Would You Know If You Have Subluxation?** Only Doctors of Chiropractic are trained and qualified to detect Vertebral Subluxation. Subluxation is commonly identified by using a combination of specific objective tests like X-ray, thermography, palpation, postural evaluation, gait analysis, leg checks, and muscle testing.

10. **What Should You Do If You Have Subluxation?** Teach your patients that subluxation can be reduced and corrected with specific Chiropractic Adjustments. Only a Chiropractic Adjustment can correct subluxation. Typically, a series of adjustments are necessary to reduce subluxation.

11. **I'm on a Mission.** Share your passion for helping people with your patients. They will be inspired by your Vision for a better tomorrow for your community. They want to be part of something meaningful—and will help you serve the Mission—if you recruit and empower them.

12. **I Need Your Help.** Teach your patients that everyone that they know has a spine and nervous system. Everyone's under tremendous stress in modern life. Most likely, a lot of the people that they know are sick and struggling, and the root cause of their problems could be subluxation. Tell them you could help them if they only knew—so this is where you need their help.

And that's the Dirty Dozen—the twelve things every patient needs to know.

So *when* and *where* do you teach these concepts? The short answer is every-where. But let's discuss my three favorite "mechanisms" (interactions built into your Patient Process so that they are guaranteed to happen). The first is **Table Talk**, your table-side patient education; the second is the **New Patient Orientation Workshop**, and finally, teach these at the periodic **Progress Exams** and **Progress Reports**.

My goal is to really focus on teaching these twelve concepts **consistently** through the first stage of care. In our model, the first stage of care is known as the Initial Intensive Care. This typically lasts three to four months. During these first months, it is critical to create a solid foundation of understanding for each patient. This is when the patient is *available* to you to learn a new way to better health, and you have the opportunity to challenge and shape their belief system for life. This is when they become Understanders.

It's important that this happens before their first care plan is complete. You want to make sure that the patient *understands* chiropractic before you ask them to recommit to the next leg of the journey.

The next step for the patient is a complete Reexamination and a new Report of Findings. I refer to this report as the patient's "Report Card." I'll explain that in a minute.

At the Re-Exam, Re-Report and Re-Commitment, it's time to revisit the Four Agreements. Make sure that the patient agrees on the Problem at this point, sets and agrees on new Goals moving forward, agrees on the new Path to achieve those goals and agrees on a new financial Plan to pay for it.

I'll suggest that you first review their original Four Agreements: where were they when they first presented (The Problem); what were they trying to accomplish (The Goals); and how were they going to get there (The Path). You can skip The Plan at this point (the original payment agreement). Then you'll go over their new findings from their exam— update them as to where they are on their journey back to health. Be sure to update their goals at this point, as well. Remember, recommendations are always based on two things: their goals and your findings (from their recent exam). Great coaches—and doctors—always keep compelling goals in front of their patients.

When it is time to give the patient their new Recommendations for Care, they face a fork in the road with three choices. Make sure that you position their choices based on **outcomes**. People buy outcomes—not features.

Ask the patient about their **goals**. What are they trying to accomplish? If they want to continue to get healthier and stronger—recommend Corrective Care. If they are happy with where they are now and wish to protect this new level of health and prevent backsliding and losing what they've gained—recommend Maintenance Care. Of course, there is a third choice. They could choose to discontinue care, but this would mean that they would be choosing to slide backwards over time and lose what they had gained.

For this to make sense to the practice member, they would need to understand the Dirty Dozen. They would have to know the causes of subluxation in their lives—the things that they do specifically—and the stresses that they face every day that cause their subluxation pattern to reoccur.

Additionally, one of the most important things to teach people is **how they can influence their clinical outcomes**. It is critical to *partner* with the patient and empower them with the strategies that give them a sense of influence—and responsibility—for the results of their chiropractic care. Make sure that your patients understand this is a partnership.

I equip my patients with the knowledge and strategies to get the best results. I love to teach **The Three-Legged Stool of Results**. The first leg is to keep their appointment schedule. Follow the doctor's recommendations for care. Do not miss or change appointments. The second leg of the stool is to break their bad habits that cause their subluxations to reoccur. The third leg is to add the specific, prescribed exercises they are given so that they can strengthen the muscles of the spine and hold their adjustments better. This empowers the patient to influence their outcomes and get better results!

In fact, I like to say that Chiropractic is a "done with you program"—not a "done for you program." This is why I refer to the Re-Exam/Re-Report as *their* Report Card—not mine.

This re-exam and new report of findings is **where the rubber meets the road**, so to speak. The stakes are high. You're looking for a full-on re-commitment from the patient.

Naturally it can be pretty nerve-wracking for the chiropractor. Did you deliver the results that the patient is expecting? Here is where you will find out. Is the patient expecting a big "Ta-Da!" moment with a perfect post X-ray? Startling postural changes? Total symptomatic resolution? What is the patient expecting at this point, and more accurately, what does the patient understand about chiropractic at this point?

> *The Re-Exam/Re-Report is the Patient's*
> *Report Card—not the Doctor's.*

It is absolutely critical that you set the patient's expectations on the front end. As I said, this is a "done with you" not "done for you" program. It's a partnership. You cannot "do an outcome" for them—but you can shepherd them through the process.

You must systematize these initial clarifying conversations as part of your process—and make sure the patient hears this from the beginning. They must hear it again table side in your Patient Education, at the workshop, and at the Progress Exams. I recommend taking a Socratic approach to teaching—asking them questions as you go, checking in on their understanding. Remind them that their Report Card is coming up. If you do this right, when it's time for the Re-exam and Re-report, you will have an Understander on your hands—someone who wants Chiropractic because they understand Chiropractic. And they will eagerly continue their care and happily follow your recommendations.

Commit to teaching the Dirty Dozen, through all of these touch-points (Table Talk, workshop, and re-progress exam/re-report), and you will succeed in turning your patients into Understanders—and greatly increase your Patient Retention.

I can't emphasize this enough: those first four months are key. Let's face it, you cannot do every day perfectly with every patient, but if you make it your goal to perform those first four months of care perfectly, you will have a patient for life.

Get those first four months right, and your patients will stay forever. They'll get the results they're looking for. You'll grow your practice. And you'll all feel fulfilled. Win-Win-Win.

## RETENTION IS A WIN-WIN-WIN

How is that possible? Let me explain. First, you've got the patient's win. We know that when they stay under regular chiropractic care and start to leverage it as a lifestyle success strategy and not just a short-term treatment for a symptom, or crisis, or condition, that's where the best results live.

We know that the best clinical outcomes come over time, and that we chiropractors do our best work over time. The longer a person is under regular chiropractic care—and stay subluxation free, with their nervous system functioning optimally—the healthier they get and the more resilient they become. There is a **Compound Effect** to staying healthy—just like there's a compound effect to staying sick.

It's amazing to witness. Through continued chiropractic care, in essence, we build these humans beings and allow them to have a full expression of their genetic potential across the nervous system over a lifetime. We see this especially in the children we care for. Children who grow up under regular chiropractic care without subluxation tend to grow up healthier and develop optimally.

All of which is to say, Retention—and the compound benefit of being under regular chiropractic care—is indeed a big win for the patient.

But it's also a big win for the practice. **Growth lives in retention**. Instead of having a revolving door—with some people coming in, some people converting to care, some people staying under care, some people dropping out—you actually create Ideal Patients and collect Ideal Patients. They're satisfied, they're getting great results, they understand chiropractic, and so they're staying. That's the **Aggregate Effect**.

Creating and collecting ideal Patients is the essence of real practice growth. And it's a great business model. Keeping happy, satisfied "consumers" is far more cost-effective than trying to replace people who drop out of care. Marketing is expensive. In fact, in most practices, if you were to double your Patient Retention you'd triple your profit.

> *If you double your Retention, you can triple your profit.*

Last but not least, retention is also a personal win for you, the doctor, and for your staff. It is incredibly *fulfilling* to see patients stay in continued care.

We all know how bad it feels, how frustrating, when a patient drops out of care. It's the worst. One minute they were *in*, part of the tribe, you were taking good care of them. The next, they're gone. That's a pain that all chiropractors can relate to.

But now, you will have the opportunity to feel the opposite. And it feels great, let me tell you, to see people stay under care and raise their families in your office. Before you know it, you're accumulating this beautiful community of folks who are like-minded, who are using similar strategies and getting better health outcomes. The aggregate effect is just so fulfilling for a doctor—and the Team.

My own practice is particularly renowned for turning Believers into Understanders, and for our success through incredible Retention. Whereas the PVA, or patient visit average, for most chiropractors is somewhere between twelve and eighteen—meaning that their average patient sees them twelve to eighteen times total—in our practice we've enjoyed a PVA above 300 for nearly fifteen years.

The average person who came to us came back more than 300 times. And that's just our average patient—many are even higher!

How do you do that? Do a really, really good job of educating people on the front end about the value of their care, and then do a great job of *delivering* the value. I studied our practice for years trying to figure out what exactly we did differently that drove our PVA so high.

Gradually, over the course of coaching thousands of other doctors, I landed on what I call The Big Seven, which are the seven things you need to make sure are in place in your practice in order to consistently create value and clarity around continued chiropractic care.

Remember: **Your Retention is a Reflection of Your Clarity.**

# THE BIG SEVEN

Why are so many of your patients dropping out of care? Here are the most common pitfalls that I see.

Number one is **Product Confusion**. You are selling one thing, but what they bought is something else entirely.

Number two is **Expectations and Agreements**. All successful long-term relationships begin with very clear expectations and agreements from both sides.

Number three is **Table Talk**, which means continued education from visit to visit—every patient interaction must include an education that challenges and shapes their belief system.

Number four: **New Patient Orientation**. Are you teaching a Patient Workshop? Is it mandatory? Are you creating a paradigm shift for your patients at the New Patient Orientation?

Number five, then, is the **Measurement Effect**, also known as the Hawthorne effect. Behavioral science tells us that humans love to be measured. This speaks to the importance of continued Progress Examinations and Progress Reports.

Number six is **Flow**. If you have flow issues in your practice, you're making it harder for your patients than it needs to be. Maybe your location sucks, or your hours, or your phone trafficking, front desk, wait time. It could be all sorts of things. But the common denominator is that there's friction.

Finally, number seven is **Value Economy**. As described at the beginning of this chapter, the patient has a scale in their brain, and they're weighing the value of continued care against the time, energy, focus, and money that they will have to invest with you in order to get what they want. As soon as they lose clarity around the value of continuing chiropractic care—they are gone.

**You have to create value and clarity for them.**

The good news is if you get things right in these seven areas, you will be successful at Retention. But remember: it's not enough to just do these things; you have to *systematize* them. Make sure you put **mechanisms** in place to capture your process so you don't have to resort to memory management.

For more on this, go here: theremarkablepractice.com/Retention.

## RETENTION IS INTELLECTUAL

The reason that retention and systematizing your Retention Process is so critically important in a chiropractic practice is that it speaks to the very essence of what we do as chiropractors.

**We want patients to adopt chiropractic as a lifestyle success strategy.**

We don't want them to just dabble in it. Staying under regular care is the whole point of chiropractic. It's the only way for our patients to experience their optimal potential—for them to enjoy Wellness.

We know that wellness is defined as our ability to adapt to stress. Our body should adapt readily and appropriately to the internal and external stressors that we constantly face. As chiropractors, we work with the spine specifically, because the spine houses and protects the nervous system. If your spine is healthy and your nervous system is functioning well, you deal with stress better.

Rather than fixating on "stress reduction" only, chiropractic helps people tolerate and adapt to the stressors that they inevitably face. When we adapt to stresses well, we stay healthy. When your patients understand this—they will want to stay under regular care. This is key to them becoming Understanders. This is the key to Retention.

Let's revisit a concept that we discussed in our Conversion study:

### Conversion Is Emotional. Retention is Intellectual.

If you recall, in the Conversion Process, we want to remember that people will *start* care based on what they *feel*. "Do I feel like I am in the right place?" That is the emotional driver of conversion. But starting care is one thing—*staying* under care (Retention) is a different thing entirely.

**People will *start* care based on what they feel—but they will *stay* under care based on what they know.**

As with Conversion, there is an 80/20 rule at play. Remember from Conversion: 80 percent of your focus (what you talk about) should be around **their story**—why they are here, what they think their problem is, the Life Effect of that problem and what they are trying to accomplish (their goals)—you know, their story. And 20 percent of the time you should be focused on our story—the Chiropractic Story. In other words, talking about the solution.

Well this flips around completely when it comes to Retention. People will start based on what they feel—but **they will stay based on what they know**. Retention is intellectual.

Once a patient converts to care, **you want to spend 80 percent of your time talking to your patients about chiropractic**. Teach them about the Wellness Paradigm, the Chiropractic Principle and help shape their new view on health and their body. You're teaching them what's possible, as well as the strategies they need to employ to get their health back—so that they know exactly what to start doing and stop doing to get the results they seek.

You should use the remaining 20 percent of your time with the patient discussing their symptoms or whatever may be going on in their life and their world.

Unfortunately, most chiropractors get this completely backward. When they're trying to convert the patient, they spend 80 percent of their time telling the person everything that they never wanted to know about chiropractic and then only 20 percent is focused on the patient and *their* story. They miss the empathetic connection entirely.

Then, when it comes time for retention—assuming the patient hasn't quit already—they spend 80 percent of their time talking about their symptom of the day and only 20 percent of the time teaching them about the things that are actually going to help the patient get the results that they want!

I know that this may feel counter-intuitive but trust me—it works. You've got to be highly intentional about this. And you cannot rely on "memory management" to do it. This is why systematizing your Retention Process is crucial.

## A FINAL WORD ON SYSTEMS

Over the past three chapters, we've outlined our proven systems for Attracting, Converting, and Retaining patients—the three operational domains of practice success.

These are the three spinning plates of practice operations, if you will. They must be fully integrated so that one feeds into the next seamlessly.

Each needs to be systematized and captured in operation manuals. They are to be embraced, trained-on and mastered. As I've stated, systems are the key to transforming your job into a business and are vital to creating a Scalable, Durable and Transferable asset.

But what I discovered over the course of over fifteen years coaching thousands of doctors was that they have as many challenges and questions, if not more, around their employees, their staff, their team. The pain points that I hear constantly involve issues with Team: "I cannot find a great CA…"I have to fire this CA…I'm losing that CA…my Office Manager is leaving to go have a baby…I cannot motivate my Team…I cannot find a good Associate Doctor…I cannot get my Associate to produce…" The "people problems" are endless.

Eventually, I came to recognize that there is in fact a fourth domain—and that's **Team Building**. In a sense, it's the most important of all: if you don't get this one right, it doesn't matter how good your systems are. **Build a great Team—or you own a job**.

Therefore, I have devoted the entire next chapter to building your team—the fourth side of the Rubik's Cube Puzzle of Success. Admittedly, the need for this information was initially a blind spot for me. But now, it is the most important work that we do. Let's dig into Team Building and help you create your own Remarkable Team.

## SUMMARY

- Retention is a Reflection of Clarity: your clarity, your Team's clarity, and your patients' clarity around the Value of continuing regular chiropractic care.
- People start care based on what they *feel*; they stay under care based on what they *know*.
- Conversion is Emotional. Retention is Intellectual.

- New Patients start care as Believers—they believe that you will get them what they want. The job of the Retention System is to turn Believers into Understanders.
- People who understand Chiropractic, want Chiropractic.
- The **Dirty Dozen** are the twelve concepts that every patient needs to know.
- The Big Seven are the mechanisms that are built into the Remarkable Practice System to ensure that Believers become Understanders

*To Download All the Chapter Resources, Go Here:*
1. theremarkablepractice.com/Retention

*To Learn More, Check Out These Remarkable Resources*
2. TRP Academy: theremarkablepractice.com/tbr-academy
3. TRP DC and CA Process and Procedure Manuals: theremarkablepractice.com/tbr-manuals
4. TRP Private Coaching: theremarkablepractice.com/tbr-coaching
5. Remarkable Live Immersion Events: theremarkablepractice. com/tbr-events

1    2    3    4    5

# CHAPTER SEVEN

# TEAM BUILDING

*"95% of your problems are people problems."*

—*Top Grading*

In the last chapter, we talked about the importance of Patient Retention, but Retention is not something that's just up to you, the doctor. The entire team must begin with that end in mind. Doctor, it is your role as "Owner"—the Leader—the CEO of your practice to cast the Vision of "what success looks like" for your Team. You must make sure that they own it so that everything that is done and said in your practice is **aligned** with Retention—with no contradictions.

This is no small task and it is up to you to establish this with your Team. Whenever you are trying to imprint something into your Team's culture—I'll suggest the **heart**, **head**, **hands** and **feet** approach to getting them on board.

Using Patient Retention as an example, it breaks down like this: the **heart** is the *why*. "Why is Retention important? Why is Retention important to the patient? Why is it important to the practice? Why is it important to me?" **I've got to feel it.**

The **head** is the *what*. "What does it look like? Let me try to wrap my head around it and really understand what we're doing. Let me close my eyes and envision it—from the highest, 30,000-feet level, then zooming into 10,000 feet, then to 1,000 feet, and finally to the ground level. What does "Remarkable Retention look like?" **I've got to see it.**

The **hands** are the *how*. "How do I do it? How do I keep my patients for life? What is the Process? The Procedure? The steps? The script?" **I've got to learn it.**

And finally, the **feet**: "Let's do it." The feet symbolize the training, the role playing. The feet represent everything you do to get your team up to speed...Let's run through it...let's go, let's grow!" **I've got to do it.**

And this is true not only for Retention but *all* the processes, procedures, and systems covered in this book. You can't be the only one who has **clarity** around this. The whole Team must be oriented toward it. It has to be in the DNA of the practice, as part of the company's culture.

The team must see that these mechanisms are in place. There has to be a visibility into all of the moving parts. And it all has to be done deliberately. It can't just be left to happenstance or memory management. This is highly intentional.

Everyone on your Team must see and understand the entire process. Your Team should know the whole narrative. They need to know what is being done and why. They need to know what is being said and why. They also need to know *their role* in making it happen—and know the role of every player on the Team.

In short, everyone has to be in sync. You can't have a team where everyone just does their own thing—focused on their job—but they don't see the forest for the trees. That would be like trying to put on a play where everyone only studies his or her own lines without any context. That play would suck, right? It would have no emotion, no story, and would be a terrible experience for the audience.

Which is why it is so incredibly important to have a team that's in sync and has been systematically oriented and aligned with one another. They learn together. They train together and they grow together. If each person is only focused on "their piece of the puzzle" your process will feel disjointed and lack context, and your results will suffer.

Building a **Remarkable Team** is as important as it is difficult. But when you make it happen, you go from owning a job to owning a business. Let's talk about getting the *right* people onto your Team.

## WHO IS ON YOUR TEAM?

According to Top Grading—the world's leading HR experts when it comes to building out your teams professionally—"*95% of your problems as a business owner are people problems.*"

As famous as that statistic has become, it still shocks. What if you could take 95 percent of your problems and make them go away?

No matter the industry, team building occupies so much of our time, energy, focus, and money. I didn't realize at first just how much of an issue it was in chiropractic. I was still so focused on coaching doctors on the three domains of practice success. "Attraction, Conversion, Retention" was my battle cry.

It wasn't until I started doing a lot of one-on-one coaching and spending time on the phone with these doctors that I heard firsthand about all the staff issues and challenges they were having around their team members. I would try to drag the conversation back on track, to the subject that I wanted to talk about—*how to build their business*. But then I stopped myself. It hit me like a lightning bolt. I had stumbled on a major blind spot as a coach and leader.

*Holy crap*, I thought. *These people don't know how to put a team together. It doesn't matter what processes, procedures, and systems I give them. If they don't have the team to execute these things, if they don't have the people in place to make this all happen,* **it's not going to work**.

> *Even with the right systems in place, if you do not have the right* **team***, it will not work.*

It was a revelation to me, because I had struggled with team building myself, but had learned to fix it. Once I did, I kind of just moved on. I didn't realize that everyone else—all these doctors I was now coaching—were experiencing the same issues.

In my case, the problem had been about training. I'm naturally a pretty good team builder, and have always been able to put together good people. But then all I was doing was hiring these nice folks—who loved chiropractic and were friendly with our patients—and putting them up front in the office. I wasn't giving them responsibilities. I certainly wasn't training and equipping them to help me execute the systems. Nor was I recruiting people who I would be able to delegate to.

Let me remind you, this was back in my Control Freak/Perfectionist/ Clydesdale Period. I wanted everything done my way, perfectly—and

I was "happy" to do it myself. As I said, this nearly killed me, wrecked my marriage and stole my joy and passion. It also capped my practice growth and success. Lose, lose, lose.

Thankfully, I recognized that I needed to start hiring people with very specific skillsets and attributes to fill very specific roles that called for them to do very specific things. All in all, I became more intuitive about the fact that I couldn't just hire folks because they were nice and available. I had to be more specific and deliberate about the people I was bringing onto my team.

Moreover, I had to stop shouldering the burden of carrying the whole thing on my back. The way I had run the business up to this point was that everyone else just had to support me, they just needed to know their part and I would handle the rest. **I was the only person who really understood the overriding narrative.** Everyone else on the team was just playing their part, their role in the play. I was the glue that held it all together, and I didn't want to be that glue anymore.

I decided to become a Team Building Expert.

Again, I came to these realizations on my own, and it made all the difference in our practice. But it wasn't until much later that I began to see all these other doctors going through the same challenges. I saw how their energy was being drained and their practice success was being stifled—all because they did not know how to build a Remarkable Team.

> *Your practice will only be as big as your Team wants it to be.*

I realized this was actually a pandemic. *Everybody* has problems with their teams. I learned that if your team is sideways, the capacity of your practice is going to be capped at 50 percent. It will only grow to about 50 percent of its potential. If you hire the wrong people—50 percent cap. If your people lack the skillsets they need—50 percent cap. If your people lack or lose the Vision or the Purpose—50 percent cap. Here's what I know: your practice will only be as big as your Team wants it to be.

Fast forward to the present, and nowadays I see the coaching I do around Team Building as the most important and most valuable contribution I could possibly be making to the chiropractic community.

## WHAT DOES SUCCESS LOOK LIKE FOR YOU AS A TEAM?

When it comes to Team Building, the first step is to do what you did at the beginning of this book and develop your Vision Story for your team. What does success look like for your team? Can you describe your ideal team? What are the positions on the team? What are the attributes of the people who would excel in those positions?

Again, you should be able to describe this vision in such a detailed, compelling way that it will make your listener *want* to help you create it. For more on this, go to: theremarkablepractice.com/People.

Then, just like you did before, look at your Core Values, but now in terms of the values of your practice. For example, maybe one of the Core Values for your practice—as a place of health and healing—is to drive better clinical outcomes.

Or maybe, your practice—as a place of patient education—has the core value of teaching and showing people a better way to better health. Maybe your core value is empathy or compassion. Maybe it's leadership. Or family. Tribe. Unconditional love. Professionalism. These are just some of the broad categories that crop up often when I do this Core Value exercise with TRP Clients.

For us, *positivity* was and is one of our most important values. It is at the very core of our practice, our team, and our culture.

### CHECK IN CA (CICA)

- THE BOSS OF TODAY
- SCHEDULE BOOK
- PATIENT FLOW
- INTERNAL PROMOTIONS
- EXTROVERT / ENERGY

### CHECK OUT CA (COCA)

- THE BOSS OF TOMORROW
- OFFICE POLICIES
- COMPLIANCE OFFICE
- PAYMENT COLLECTIONS
- INTROVERT / DETAILS

### TECH CA (TECA)

- CLINICAL ASSISTANT
- NEW PATIENT CONCIERGE
- INTERNAL SALES FORCE
- NP CONVERSION
- EMPATHETIC CONNECTOR

### BACK OFFICE CA (BOCA)

- BUSINESS OFFICE MGT
- ACCOUNTS AND INSURANCE
- PAYROLL / MAIL / BANKING
- SYSTEMS AND ORGANIZATION
- DETAILS ORIENTED / ORGANIZED

### OFFICE MANAGER / COO / INTEGRATOR

- LEADERSHIP TEAM
- RUNS THE BUSINESS
- LMA: LEADERSHIP, MANAGEMENT, ACCOUNTABILITY
- ACCOUNTABILITY CHART, SCORECARDS, KPI'S
- ORGANIZED, DRIVEN, FOCUSED

### NEW BUSINESS DEVELOPMENT EXPERT (NBDE)

- PROFESSIONAL SALES PERSON
- NETWORKS ON YOUR BEHALF
- DEVELOPS RELATIONSHIPS TO LEVERAGE INTO EXTERNAL MARKETING EVENTS
- OUTSIDE TALKS, SPINAL SCREENINGS, CORPORATE WELLNESS
- OUTGOING, EXTROVERT, SALES PROFESSIONAL

### SENIOR DC (EX: BUSINESS BUILDER)

- CEO / VISIONARY
- WIN / WIN
- LEADS THE TEAM
- NEW BUSINESS DEVELOPMENT
- CLINIC DIRECTOR

### JUNIOR / ASSOCIATE DC (EX: CARE GIVER)

- PATIENT CARE / CLINICAL
- PATIENT EDUCATION / PROMOTION
- VALUE CREATION AND DELIVERY
- CLARITY DEVELOPMENT AND RETENTION
- ASSIST IN NP CONVERSION / RECONVERSION

## YOU HIRE AND FIRE BY YOUR CORE VALUES

As you consider your own Core Values for *your* practice, take the time to get this right. What you come up with is the granite foundation of your practice and the team you are building. These Core Values are going to shape how you practice, who you attract as patients and who you hire and fire along the way.

To be clear, while your **Vision Story** for your Team may change at certain inflection points through the seasons of your life and career, your **Core Values** should stay the same.

**You should be able to get a forearm tattoo of your practice's Core Values**. That's how rock solid they should be. They *have* to be, in order for you to hire people who are representative of and *aligned* with those values. Really, your team should be an expression or manifestation of your business's Core Values: theremarkablepractice.com/People.

When you advertise for those positions and when you interview candidates, you're going to want to make sure that they are in line with your practice's values. This is critically important. More on finding and hiring your ideal team members in a moment.

But before you get to that point, you must first create your **Organizational Chart**. This "Org Chart" is the classic flowchart showing all the different positions on your team. Then, under each position you're going to have a box where you can write the Team Members name who is currently manning that position. See the example on the following page.

Once you have completed your Org Chart, it's time to start fleshing out the Job Roles and Responsibilities. It will look a bit like an abbreviated, bulleted job description. You should include three bullets for each position. These bullets should be considered the primary responsibilities of that position. Try to resist the urge to create "Roles" based on a person who is already on your Team. Rather, imagine that you are fielding a football team. Draw out all of the positions...Quarterback, Running Back, Center, Tight End, Wide Receiver, Kicker...etc. Summarize their role in three bullets. Examples for the football quarterback may be:

- Call the Plays
- Complete Passes
- Protect the Ball

The three bullets for you as the CEO/Clinic Director/Owner may be as follows:

- Vision cast for the team and practice
- Deliver clinical excellence (educate and adjust patients)
- Train and develop the team

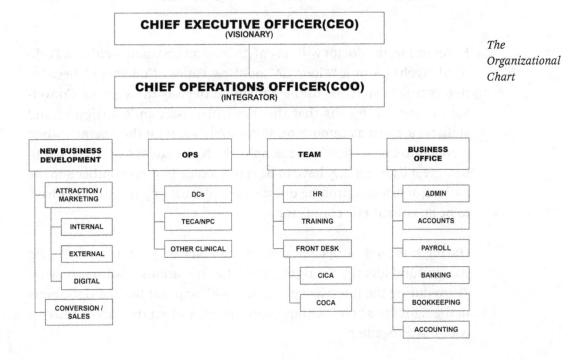

*The Organizational Chart*

Capture these bulleted job descriptions on your Organizational Chart and it now becomes an **Accountability Chart**. See example below.

For example, the doctor will very often have an assistant—either a Technical (Tech) CA or a "Floor CA" or "New Patient Concierge." Because this person is attached to the patient all the way through the Conversion Process, it means that this particular assistant's attributes and skillsets are just as important, if not more so, than the doctor's when it comes to Conversion. For example, the New Patient Concierge has to be a great listener; they have to be very Socratic in their approach to the patient, able to ask probing questions; and most importantly, they have to be an **empathetic connector**.

Having this level of insight around the Roles on your Team will help you find and identify the right person for the various positions on your Team during the interview process. It will help you put the right butts in the right seats "on your bus" so to speak. And get the wrong butts off your bus altogether.

Which brings up the uglier side of Team Building. So many DCs that I talk to are frustrated because they know that they do not have the right people on their Team. Either they have gaps, but they are afraid to hire and screw it up. Or they do not want to add the overhead expense. Or they are terrified to fire someone who does not belong because they feel unequipped to replace them. This is a terrible place to lead from and creates a bad energy and attitude in the practice. Some docs actually feel like they are held hostage by their Team. A "staff infection" will kill a business. And it's usually a slow and painful death. Let's fix these issues now.

Next, all the information from the chart needs to get organized into what we call **Scorecards**. There are Scorecards for each Team Member (**Individual Scorecard**\*): like a powerful dashboard that helps them stay focused.

Remember: **focus** is the difference between busyness and productivity. Every Teams is busy, with lots of particle movement, lots of stuff moving around. You want yours to be productive. Scorecards create *focus* for everyone on your Team.

> *Focus is what makes the difference between busyness and productivity.*

Every quarter, team members will get a new scorecard with five **KPIs** or **Key Performance Indictors**. These are the five metrics or statistics that they own. These are the five things that they are individually accountable for—these are the metrics and activities that they are to focus on this quarter. Accountability doesn't just mean doing what they are tasked to do, but also reporting back to the rest of the group. Keeping this number on track and in front of mind for the Team.

---

\* *Inspired by Gino Wickman's Scorecard from his book Traction.*

For each metric or KPI, there is a **Benchmark**, which is where that metric is at the start of that quarter, as well as the **Goal** for that metric for the end of the quarter. Most importantly, there is the specific **Activity** that this particular Team Member is to focus on—an activity which will predictably drive that "stat" from the Benchmark toward the Goal.

From then on, the KPIs become the focus point of all conversation moving forward. When you're at a team meeting, everyone reports on their KPIs. When you do your Monthly Meet-Ups, each Team Member reports on their KPIs. When you have your Quarterly Reviews, you talk about the KPIs. *They are the center of the conversation.*

> *The Scorecard is the foundation of the Expectations and Agreements that you form with each Team Member.*

When it comes down to it, your team members' **Scorecards are the foundation of your entire relationship** with them. Think about it this way: the scorecard is a physical manifestation of the concept of setting Expectations and Agreements—and Expectations and Agreements are key to *any* successful long-term relationship.

You will, of course, also use the Scorecards to help your Team with their **Goal Setting**. First, as the CEO of the Business, you will set the Goals for the organization. From there, you can set individual Team Member Goals—and help them gain clarity around their specific contribution to achieving those goals. Give them the opportunity to "chime in" on these goals and take ownership of them. Like Daniel Pink says, "Chime-In begets Buy-In."

To clarify, the initial goal-setting exercise is for the *whole practice*—we like to use Jim Collins' *Good to Great* model of the BHAG, the Big Hairy Audacious Goal for the end of the year, and the NHAG, which is the Next Happily Achievable goal—but then the scorecards are where it becomes really personal to each individual team member.

# TRP SCORECARD: INDIVIDUAL

*Scorecard—Individual*

| Team Member: | | Primary Objectives |
|---|---|---|
| Position: | | 1. |
| Date: ___/___/___ | | 2. |
| Quarter: ( ) _____ | | 3. |

**Top 5 Priorities**

| | KPI | Key Performance Indicator | Benchmark | Goal | Result | Action Item |
|---|---|---|---|---|---|---|
| 1 | | | | | | |
| 2 | | | | | | |
| 3 | | | | | | |
| 4 | | | | | | |
| 5 | | | | | | |

**Monthly Meet-Up**

| | | Month 1 | | Month 2 | | Month 3 | |
|---|---|---|---|---|---|---|---|
| | KPI | Status | Notes | Status | Notes | Result | Notes |
| 1 | | | | | | | |
| 2 | | | | | | | |
| 3 | | | | | | | |
| 4 | | | | | | | |
| 5 | | | | | | | |

Status:   (+) = Ahead   (Δ) = On Track   (-) = Behind

For more on this, go here: theremarkablepractice.com/People.

The Scorecard is a *living, working document*. **It is a tool that you will use to create clarity and accountability.** You'll have individual monthly meet-ups (just fifteen minutes each) with each Team Member to talk about their Scorecard and update it.

I suggest establishing a **Meeting Rhythm** as follows:

First, you have your **Board Meetings.** These are inspirational quarterly Team meetings that cover four critical elements: **Vision Casting, Product and Process, Goal Setting** and **Marketing.** (See the first four modules in the Remarkable Practice Academy.) I suggest that you do "full" Board Meetings every other quarter (i.e., first and third quarters) and "mini" Board Meetings on the alternating quarters (i.e., second and fourth) where you simply review the Goals and Marketing Plan and Calendar. In addition, you should hold individual **Quarterly Reviews** with each Team Member. This is where new Scorecards with KPI's and goals for that individual are established and agreed upon. Then there are the **Individual Monthly Meet-Ups**, which are done on day thirty, day sixty, leading up to day ninety, which is the next Quarterly Review.

Zooming in to a micro level, you've also got your **Weekly Team Meetings**, **Team Trainings**, and **Daily Huddles**, which I call Pre-Shift and Post-Shift Huddles.

For **Meeting Form** and **Huddle Sheet**, go here: theremarkablepractice. com/People.

Those are your Meeting Rhythms, and therefore those are also your *communication* rhythms. The Scorecard becomes a focal point of all those exchanges or collisions. Again, the importance of the Scorecard cannot be overstated. Honestly, getting the Scorecards right for your Team may take two or three quarters—it's a lot of work. But once these are in place, you will enjoy a level of focus and productivity that you have never experienced. **Scorecards make the difference between owning a job and owning a business.**

So now you have your Organization Chart and Accountability Chart created—the "blueprint" for your Vision Story of a Successful Practice. And you now understand the importance of Scorecards and how these create focus, accountability, and productivity. You've established a Meeting Rhythm culture and you have a Reporting System in place to keep things objective. Now it's time to build your own Remarkable Team. Now it's time to talk about the Team-Building Process: Finding and Interviewing; Hiring and Onboarding; Training and Equipping and Developing and Retaining Remarkable Team Members.

So how then do you go about *finding* these people?

## FINDING AND HIRING, INTERVIEWING AND ONBOARDING

When we talk about finding CAs, there are a few different methodologies. There's the "done by you," the "done with you," and the "done for you."

What's most important, especially if you're the one doing the finding yourself, is that you be super clear about who it is you're looking for. Who does your team need right now? You have to know the positions on your team, the attributes of the individuals who would excel in those positions, and where the gaps are.

Think about it like you own a sports franchise. If you were building a basketball team, you know you'd need a center, a power forward, a shooting forward, a shooting guard, a point guard.

It may sound like common sense, but the truth is, nobody in our industry operates like this. They hire people who they like and who are available.

I encourage you to think about hiring in a much more strategic way.

I believe that God only makes geniuses. Our job as the CEO is to put every Team Member in the position that calls for them to work in their genius.

## THREE-LEGGED STOOL OF HIRING

We utilize a Three-Legged Stool approach to the Hiring Process: Objective (testing), Subjective (interview process) and Historical (a review of work history and references).

A deep dive on our Interview Process is outside the scope of this book—but it may be an excellent topic for a sequel. For now, let's double-click on one leg of this process: Objective Testing.

When hiring, you want to consider three different parts of the mind: **cognitive**, **affective**, and **conative**. The first, cognitive, looks at what the applicant *knows*. What have they learned in their academic and professional lives? The second, affective, looks at what they *love*—what naturally energizes them and turns them on? Finally, the conative brain examines how they *behave*.

Too often, we neglect this last part. As my friend and business partner, Dr. Allen Miner from Chiro Match Makers (a specialized placement agency for hiring Chiropractors and Team Members) likes to say, *"We hire for skills, but we fire for behavior."* Wouldn't it be better if we could actually predict how they will act or take action? Imagine if you knew ahead of time the "blood type" of the person that will excel and thrive in a given role—and then have the ability to test an applicant to see if they are a "match"—before you move forward in the interview or hiring process. Well you can.

You do it with **objective testing**. I find the most valuable test in the hiring process is the one that actually analyzes the conative part of the brain that measures behavior—dominance, extroversion, patience, compliance, and energy. Obviously, these are five characteristics that are very important to know about a person before you hire them.

Now, of course these tests don't take the place of interviewing, but they do help to catch things you might miss. I know I have blind spots when it comes to interviewing. I love everybody and think I can fix anybody. But that doesn't necessarily mean I should hire them. That is precisely why you should objectively test first and make sure that they are hardwired to succeed in the specific role for which you are hiring. Then interview those people who are the right "blood type" only.

Testing is where things become much, much more accurate. It makes it much more likely that you will predictably find the right people. Some of these tests have been around for decades and they're very hard to game. It's important to note that discrimination laws are very specific around the legality of testing and the sequencing of tests in the hiring process. This is another reason why it is advisable to consult with a placement expert like CMM.

In combination with the interviews, tests can help make sure there's **alignment** between the candidate or applicant and your practice's needs and Core Values. Remember, whenever you're hiring somebody, you're hiring their energy, their attitude, their work ethic. It's a lot more than just their skillset.

Learn more about **Chiro Match Makers**'s testing and placement process here: theremarkablepractice.com/tbr-cmm.

Having read this chapter, you are already so much more aware. You know how to approach this thorny puzzle of team-building success. You've already come a long way on the people side—the Team side—in this journey of building a Remarkable Practice as Part of a Remarkable Life.

> *Having a Remarkable Team makes the difference*
> *between owning a job and owning a business.*

Once you have found an Ideal Match for the position for which you are hiring, the next crucial step is to **Onboard** them properly. This is a science unto itself. The Onboarding Process ensures that every new hire lands well and starts strong—and is a leading factor in determining if they stay on for the long haul. This is when we establish a full understanding around Practice Vision, Core Values, Culture and set Expectations and Agreements around every role on your Team.

Onboard your people properly or you will be faced with crippling employee turnover which is a derailer for any business.

# 10 STEPS TO ON-BOARDING A NEW CA HIRE

### NP ORIENTATION WORKSHOP

Have every new CA Hire attend your NPO "Better Results Faster Workshop" immediately. It is best to make this a first step in your interview process.

### NEW HIRE ORIENTATION

Leverage the New Hire Orientation Culture Deck to review and showcase the key cultural elements that make your practice Remarkable!

### EXPECTATIONS & AGREEMENTS REVIEW

Use the Practice Time Value Accounts to do the comprehensive review of the working parts of each category of the practice. This is a Job Description conversation.

### TRP SCORE CARD

Use the TRP Score Card to outline the Top 3 Objectives and the Top 5 Priorities/Action Steps for each Team Member. This is a critical step to outline the most important FOCUS STEPS: Responsibilities, Key Performance Indicators (Key Metrics), Baseline Goals and Bonus Structure.

### NP EXPERIENCE

Take every new CA Hire through their own New Patient Process. This is NOT a training exercise - this is THEIR OWN NP EXPERIENCE. Make sure that they personally have their own EPIPHANY.

the
**REMARKABLE**
practice

# 10 STEPS TO ON-BOARDING A NEW CA HIRE

### PROCESS AND PROCEDURE MANUAL

Equip every new CA hire with their own Process and Procedure Manual. This manual will be the key reference point for their training immediately.

### TRP CA ACADEMY

Grant access to the TRP CA Training Academy. This video training resource is a critical component of their ongoing training and cross-references the CA Process and Procedures Training Manual.

### CA COMPETENCY CHECKLIST

Make sure every CA is assigned a Competency Checklist. This will outline their Training Curriculum and serve as an accountability mechanism to track their training progress. Set train schedule, day and time. Non-negotiable attendance, preparation and performance (Role Play).

### TRP CA SUPPORT CALLS

Make sure that every CA is scheduled to be listening to and interacting on the CA Support Calls. Utilize the "Take Aways and Action Steps" Reporting PDF. Have them report at the Team Meeting what they learned on the calls and any actions they suggest your practice begin to implement. (Accountability)

### 7 DAY CA PROGRAM

Start every New CA Hire with the 7 Day CA Training Program. This series is designed specifically to be a great starting point for any new hire or CA that is new to the Chiropractic Practice or the TRP System.

The Remarkable Practice teaches a ten-step process for onboarding new Team Members. Check out the video module to learn more: *theremarkablepractice.com/People*.

As I said, this Team Building Process has four distinct steps. You are now familiar with the first two—1.) Finding and Interviewing, and 2.) Hiring and Onboarding—and are ready to advance. In chapter eight, you will learn how to 3.) Train and Equip Remarkable Team Members, and finally, how to 4.) Develop and Retain them.

## SUMMARY

- Team Building is the Fourth Domain of Practice Success.
- Systems are nearly useless without the right Team in place.
- There are four separate and unique skills and systems required for building a Remarkable Team:
  - Finding and Interviewing Remarkable Team Members
  - Hiring and Onboarding Remarkable Team Members
  - Training and Equipping Remarkable Team Members
  - Developing and Retaining Remarkable Team Members
- To Build a Team, you must know the Roles and Responsibilities around every Core Function of your business.
- An Organizational Chart defines how your business is structured.
- An Accountability Chart defines how your business runs.
- Every team member has an individual scorecard that contains their Roles and Responsibilities, Key Performance Indicators (KPIs) and Goals.
- Scorecards create FOCUS for the quarter.
- You must establish a Meeting Rhythm that includes Quarterly Board Meetings and Reviews, Monthly Meet-Ups, Weekly Team Meetings, and Daily Huddles.
- Build a Remarkable Team or you own a J-O-B.

*To Download All the Chapter Resources, Go Here:*
1. theremarkablepractice.com/People

*To Learn More, Check Out These Remarkable Resources*
2. TRP Academy: theremarkablepractice.com/tbr-academy
3. TRP DC and CA Process and Procedure Manuals: theremarkablepractice.com/tbr-manuals
4. TRP Private Coaching: theremarkablepractice.com/tbr-coaching
5. Remarkable Live Immersion Events: theremarkablepractice.com/tbr-events

1          2          3          4          5

# CHAPTER EIGHT

# TRAINING

*"Train your team or smash your head
against the wall. Your choice."*
—Dr. Stephen Franson

In chapter seven we looked at finding and interviewing Remarkable Team Members, as well as hiring and onboarding them—and developing systems for each of these processes. Now, we turn our attention to **Training** your Remarkable Team, the fifth side of the Rubik's Cube Puzzle of Practice Success.

Let's quickly review what you've learned about building out your Remarkable Team. At this point, you have already identified the roles on your team, the responsibilities of those roles, and the skillsets and attributes required for them to be executed on a high level. (Use your **Organizational Chart** and **Accountability Chart** to do this exercise.)

You've assessed and made sure the person you've put in that position is the right person. As Jim Collins taught us in *Good to Great*, make sure you have the right butts in the right seats. If not, you've moved people around and got the right butts in the right seats.

Next, you've looked at your practice and asked yourself if you have any **gaps** on your team. Is anybody missing? Do we have the specific person that has the specific attributes that a specific role calls for? If not, let this inform your next hire.

Then, you must ask one of the most important (and challenging questions): Do you have a "staff infection?" Meaning, is there anyone on the team who shouldn't be there? Is there someone filling a role on your Team that does not belong? Is there someone who does not share or represent your business's Core Values?

At this point, everyone on your Team should be situated on the Org Chart, with each role's respective responsibilities fleshed out—you now have an Accountability Chart. Next step is to complete Scorecards for every Team Member to set Expectations and Agreements. Now it's all about **Training and Equipping** them to do their best work.

In the last chapter, we talked about the importance of meetings (weekly Team Meetings, quarterly reviews, individual monthly meet-ups, etc.)—and while those are indeed important, let me be clear that *Meetings are not Trainings, and Trainings are not Meetings*. If anything, we need fewer meetings and more trainings. The only reason we see practices needing so many meetings is that they *don't* do enough training!

> *Training implies Role-Playing...*
> *otherwise you just had a meeting.*

Why is training so incredibly vital? We know that human beings flourish in a workplace when they feel that they are equipped and supported—and when they are engaged in work that is meaningful to them. Toward this end, it is essential that we give them feedback—feedback that is either recognizing them or edifying them, rewarding or correcting them. People flourish in environments where there is a level of accountability and reportability to performance.

As Daniel Pink wrote in his excellent book Drive, the key to building a great team is the acronym "A-M-P" (Autonomy, Mastery, and Purpose). In other words, people want to feel like they "own" their position, that they are trained and equipped to be excellent at it and that they are doing meaningful work for a greater Purpose. If you can give your Team these three things, they will stay AMP'd!

I love the AMP'd idea and I think it's a perfect description of how to run a great Chiropractic Team. You don't want to micromanage your Team. You want them to own their position, take responsibility for it and feel a sense of autonomy in it.

As a CEO, you want to help them master their job by investing in training, equipping, and developing them. Constantly and deliberately instill in them a sense of Purpose. Keep them mindful of the greater "why" in their work. We chiropractors tend to be a very purpose-driven bunch already, but now is the time—when it comes to training—to really practice what we preach and put in place a culture of training, with systems and processes to support it. Remember The Remarkable Practice construct: Heart, Head, Hands, Feet!

How do we do that?

# TRAINING 101

First and foremost, you've got to have your systems—of Attraction, Conversion, and Retention—defined and captured in a manual. Your manual must be current, or it is irrelevant. You've got to be able to have the Gold Standard written down so that you can say, "Look, this is how we do it here."

*The Seven Remarkable Practice Manuals*

For more information on the TRP Manuals, go to the link below: theremarkablepractice.com/tbr-manuals.

Number two: you must have the necessary **resources** available to train your team. Resources refer not only to the manual, but also videos and more. In our practice, we have a whole video library, with 300+ videos capturing the entire scope of our systems—every step of every process for both the Assistants and the Associate Doctors—for all the operational domains of our business. To learn more about the Remarkable Practice Academy, go here: http://theremarkablepractice.com/tbr-academy.

But books and videos aren't enough. You also must have support, in the form of in-house, **live trainings** for your team.

Then, you need a *curriculum* to follow and a training *schedule*. You have to actually block off real time for this. It must be scheduled—and always happen—same day, same time, every week. If you don't create the necessary space for it to happen, I can tell you now: it ain't going to happen. Here is an example of our practice schedule, including our Training Times.

*Practice Schedule Example*

| 🕐 | Monday | Tuesday | Wednesday | Thursday | Friday | Saturday |
|---|---|---|---|---|---|---|
| 6:45 | Pre-Shift Huddle | Pre-Shift Huddle | | Pre-Shift Huddle | | |
| 7:00 | | | | | | |
| 7:15 | | | | | | |
| 7:30 | | | OFFICE CLOSED | | OFFICE CLOSED | OFFICE CLOSED |
| 7:45 | Adjusting & New Patients Day 1 | Adjusting & New Patients Day 1 | | Adjusting & New Patients Day 1 | | |
| 8:00 | | | | | | |
| 8:15 | | | | | | |
| 8:30 | | | | | | |
| 8:45 | | | | | | |
| 9:00 | | | | | | |
| 9:15 | | | | | | |
| 9:30 | | | | | | |
| 9:45 | Report Time Day 2 (R1/2/3) | Report Time Re-Commitment (R4/5) | | Report Time Day 2 (R1/2/3) | | |
| 10:00 | | | | | | |
| 10:15 | | | | | | |
| 10:30 | | | Marketing Shift | | Marketing Shift | Marketing Shift |
| 10:45 | | | | | | |
| 11:00 | | | | | | |
| 11:15 | Adjusting & New Patients Day 1 | | | Adjusting & New Patients Day 1 | | |
| 11:30 | | | | | | |
| 11:45 | | | | | | |
| 12:00 | | | | | | |
| 12:15 | Post Shift Huddle | Post Shift Huddle | | Post Shift Huddle | | |
| 12:30 | | | | | | |
| 12:45 | OFFICE CLOSED | BRF Workshop Alternating Weeks* | | OFFICE CLOSED | | |
| 13:00 | | | | | | |
| 13:15 | | | OFFICE CLOSED | | | |
| 13:30 | | | | | | |
| 13:45 | | | | | | |
| 14:00 | Team Meeting | Team Training | Team Training | Marketing Meeting | | |
| 14:15 | | | | | | |
| 14:30 | | | | | | |
| 14:45 | Pre-Shift Huddle | | Pre-Shift Huddle | Pre-Shift Huddle | | |
| 15:00 | | | | | | |
| 15:15 | | | | | | |
| 15:30 | Adjusting & New Patients Day 1 | | Adjusting & New Patients Day 1 | Adjusting & New Patients Day 1 | OFFICE CLOSED | OFFICE CLOSED |
| 15:45 | | | | | | |
| 16:00 | | | | | | |
| 16:15 | | Marketing Shift | | | | |
| 16:30 | | | | | | |
| 16:45 | Report Time Day 2 (R1/2/3) | | Report Time Day 2 (R1/2/3) | Report Time Re-Commitment (R4/5) | | |
| 17:00 | | | | | | |
| 17:15 | | | | | | |
| 17:30 | Adjusting & New Patients Day 1 | | Adjusting & New Patients Day 1 | Adjusting & New Patients Day 1 | | |
| 17:45 | | | | | | |
| 18:00 | | | | | | |
| 18:15 | Post Shift Huddle | | Post Shift Huddle | Post Shift Huddle | | |
| 18:30 | | | | | | |
| 18:45 | | | BRF Workshop Alternating Weeks* | | | |
| 19:00 | | | | | | |
| 19:15 | | | | | | |

Finally, it's important to create a **Training Culture**, where training is paramount. In our practice, we like to say that: *"We see patients between trainings."* I got that from a great chiro from Hawaii, Dr. Bruce Wong, and I thought it captured the idea of a training culture perfectly.

It's not enough to just do a training session once in a while. In my experience running and observing some of the most successful practices in the world, the real businesses live and breathe training. If you do, you will be well on your way to equipping your people to excel. Training assures quality and consistency. Training creates freedom and peace of mind. And training creates **Scalability** and **Durability**.

If you do not train, then you will own a J-O-B.

## DEVELOPING AND RETAINING

Once you find and hire great team members, onboard and train them, it's essential that you keep with it and *continue* to develop them—indefinitely. It's the only way to ensure they stay with you—so that you don't have the turnover problem that plagues so many practices. Think about it, when you find an environment that helps you to continually develop as a person and a professional, when and why would you leave? This is particularly true for A-Players.

Remember that the principle of retention applies not only to patients but also to the team—and that **retention is a reflection of clarity**. Therefore, you must create greater clarity for your Team as well, especially given that your employees are the ones who interact most with the patients, often even more than the doctor. Specifically, they must have real clarity around the value of starting care—and staying under care.

Your Team must be able to answer your patients' questions. Beyond making sure that your people know how to do their job, part of **developing** them is helping them become excellent communicators—and eventually influential leaders in their own right.

Remember, developing your people is a *win for you* too. The time that you spend developing your Team members creates freedom for you. For example, I like to think that every hour that I spend developing an Associate Doctor, equals a day off for me. Put in five hours of developing that AD, and it means a week's vacation! That's a great return on my investment of time on the front end. And that's what this is all about, right? That's what we're after: a Remarkable Practice as Part of a Remarkable *Life*, getting to spend more time with your family, etc. Well, the best way to achieve all that, the best leverage you have, is from developing your people.

> *The best "R.O.T." (Return on Time Invested) is
> in Training and Developing your Team.*

## THE HIGHEST AND BEST USE OF YOUR TIME

Most business owners say that they are not developing their people because they think that they are too busy. They say they don't have the time to do it right and develop them properly.

I've heard it time and again—and what I tell people is that **the reason they think they *can't* do it is exactly why they *must* do it**. In other words, the reason they're so busy is that they're doing everything themselves! It's a self-fulfilling prophecy, and the only way out of this never-ending loop is to finally do it right and take the time to train and develop their team.

It's time for them to put in place the necessary *systems* to develop their team. And again, all their processes and procedures, scripting, and more, must be captured in a current manual.

Finally, it's time to get rid of any "staff infections." If you're holding back from developing your team because, deep down, you feel like you don't have the right people on the team—and you don't want to invest the time and energy into developing the people you do have— then that's indicative of a bigger problem. **You're being held hostage by your team.**

### *Do you have a "Staff Infection?"*

Again, you're in a Catch-22. You know it's time for so-and-so to leave the company but you're terrified to have to replace them because the devil you know is better than the one you don't know. Maybe this person is the only one who knows how to run the front desk, and they've created this bird's nest of a system in their role.

On your part, you have no idea where you would even find somebody else to rehire, how you would go about onboarding them, training and developing them. Again, the only way out of this dead end is to start doing things differently. Get clear on your Vision—what does success look like? Systematize everything. Find and hire A-Players only. And then, invest in training and developing your Team.

It's your job to do that, for your own good and your team's. Help walk them along their path. Make sure they stay On-Purpose. Create inspiring environments where they can develop further. Keep them engaged and learning by investing in seminars and online forums where they can connect with other motivated, like-minded Teams. In today's day and age, it is easier than ever to connect CAs and office managers with their peers where they can interact and share best practices virtually.

Most important, these communities, online and live, make them feel like they're part of a tribe—which helps develop them further.

Support your people in all of these areas and you will create an environment where, trust me, people will never want to leave you. As long as you keep them engaged, they will stand by you. People don't leave their jobs because of money. They leave when they become disengaged—when they feel like they're not doing meaningful work anymore, or they're bored to death, or they're not appreciated.

How do you keep those things from happening? As we will see in the following chapter, an energized Team is the key. Where there's energy, there tends to be happiness and Purpose within a team. An energized practice recognizes and celebrates its people. An energized practice makes sure everyone on the team stays attached to the Vision. An energized practice has an energized Team. And an energized Team will help grow your business.

Train and develop your people and make sure they stay engaged in the practice, and you will retain your best Team Players. An engaged Team is what will drive the energy of the practice. And as we'll see in the final chapter, **your practice is a reflection of your energy.**

## SUMMARY

- Training your people is the highest and best use of your time as a business.
- Training creates Scalability and Durability.
- Train your Team or you own a job.
- You must establish a Training Culture.
- Trainings must happen regularly and be built into a Practice Schedule.
  - Your Team will need the appropriate resources to train: Written Manuals
  - Video Trainings
  - Live Trainings (Inside your practice)
  - Live Trainings / Seminars (Outside of your practice)

- Use the Heart, Head, Hands and Feet construct:
  - Heart: Start with WHY.
  - Head: They must be able to "see WHAT it looks like."
  - Hands: Show them HOW to do it.
  - Feet: (Role-Play) They must DO it.

*To Download All the Chapter Resources, Go Here*
1. theremarkablepractice.com/training
2. TRP DC and CA Process and Procedure Manuals: theremarkablepractice.com/tbr-manuals

*To Learn More, Check Out These Remarkable Resources*
3. TRP Academy: theremarkablepractice.com/tbr-academy
4. Remarkable Private Coaching: theremarkablepractice.com/tbr-coaching
5. Remarkable Live Immersion Events: theremarkablepractice.com/tbr-events

1          2          3          4          5

## CHAPTER NINE

# ENERGY

*"Your Practice is a Reflection of Your Energy."*
—Dr. Stephen Franson

Energy is a more nebulous concept than the ones we've covered in the book so far, but that doesn't make it any less important. And because I'm The Systems Guy, I always try to systematize everything, even **Energy**.

What exactly do we mean by energy here? It's *your* energy as a doctor, it's your team's energy, and frankly, it's your patients' energy as well. Again, your practice is a reflection of your energy...

> *If the energy is up, the practice is up.*
> *If the energy is flat, the practice is flat.*
> *If the energy is down, the practice is down.*

Think of your practice as a living organism. It's an energetic thing. If you're the owner of the practice, that makes you the CEO (**Chief Energy Officer**), and it's your responsibility to be constantly aware of the energy level, always monitoring. You should be able to walk into the room and "take the temperature" of the practice's energy and influence it at will.

As Chief Energy Officer, you should also have a good sense of what you want the energy to be. Is this a high-paced activity in the practice that calls for high-energy like Adjusting Prime Time Hours? Or is it a slower-paced time that requires greater presence and focus—like a New Patient Report of Findings? It's more about just having a sixth sense and being able to modulate the energy and to set the appropriate energy for a given activity.

It's not magic. But it does require a certain skillset. The way I put it, the energy of your practice should be like the accelerator pedal underneath your foot, with you driving the practice.

## THE ENERGY EQUATION

Energy is everything. Which is why I see it as the sixth and final side of the Rubik's Cube Puzzle of Success. You could have the right Vision, the best Systems, the top People and excellent Training processes and resources—but if your **energy**—*or your Team's energy* is off—you're all done.

Because energy is so critical, I wanted to create a way to assess and influence the practice energy real-time. I wanted to put this into a system—or formula—an equation. It looks like this:

## *E = mc2*
## *Energy = Money X Crucial Communications.*

I arrived at this formula as I was trying to figure out how to create a process and system around influencing the practice energy. What I was looking for was a way to consciously audit the practice, check in on the Team, and identify where we needed to jump on the accelerator pedal—and get the energy right.

Energy = Money X Crucial Communications. Let's break this down. We've already talked about the E: energy. What about the M? **Money.** Money is great. Everybody needs money to meet their needs, to pay their bills and have a sense of security. They also want to know that there's some reward for the work they're putting in.

All of which is to say, money matters. It's important. In any business, the money has to be set up properly. There must be fair exchange. It is important that your team feels like they are being compensated fairly and that the **incentives are aligned**. They must have trust that as the practice grows, they will see greater reward. As the tide comes in, all boats will rise. Money is an effective energizer.

So going back to the equation, in order to increase energy you have to increase one or both of the multipliers. So, what are your options? You can increase the money, but money's expensive. And people tend to metabolize the effect of money: if you just increase someone's salary, somehow the excitement seems to wear off very quickly. They get over it, they get used to it. In fact—they simply begin to expect it.

Yes, sometimes companies use money to inspire more energy from their people. It works. But like I said, it's expensive. In our case, it makes more sense to leverage the other multiplier: **Crucial Communications**.

# WHAT ARE CRUCIAL COMMUNICATIONS?

I love Crucial Communications. They are readily available. They're infinitely divisible. And they're free.

When you look at these Crucial Communications as a CEO leading a team—someone who's looking to increase the energy of your practice—I'd suggest that you master the five major categories of Crucial Communications and leverage all of them.

The first is **Vision Casting**. Vision casting is about keeping the heart engaged, and making sure everybody on the team is attached to the bigger "*Why*," the purpose of the practice. You have to keep them clear on the Vision of Success, the Better Tomorrow that you are creating together and the Purpose behind all the energy you're asking them to put in. Where there is a compelling Vision, there is energy...and "where there is no Vision, the people perish."

Then there are **Expectations and Agreements**. Setting expectations and agreements is about making sure everyone understands their specific role and responsibilities in helping the practice create that Better Tomorrow. You want your people to have real clarity about how they can contribute, what's expected of them, how their success is being measured, and how they can influence their outcomes. In other words, what do they need to do to succeed? Clarity creates energy—and energy drives productivity.

Third, we have **Training and Equipping**. Now that you've painted the vision for your team and set expectations and agreements around their roles in creating that vision, you must train and equip them to be excellent at their work. This is the part that involves investing time, energy, focus, and money into developing your team. Investing in training your people energizes them and builds your business faster than any other dollar you could spend.

Fourth is **Guardrails and Discipline**. Guardrails are when you set up certain policies around being an employee or a patient. They are your rules of engagement. They explain how you operate and what it means to be a Team Member.

Discipline, then, is what has to happen when someone steps outside these guardrails. You have to call them on it, and if they don't reconcile, you have to release them. Let them go do something else. Get them off the team. When someone on your Team is out of integrity—everyone knows it—and it will suck the energy out of the room if you as the leader do not take action and fix it.

The fifth and final Crucial Communication: **Recognition and Celebration**. This one is my favorite—and is arguably the most powerful.

**Recognition** is more about individual behavior. It's about catching someone doing something right and pointing it out in a genuine and authentic way. It must be timely, specific, and personal, and you have to recognize the person in a way that they will appreciate. (Each Team Member will have their own "Love Language" as to how they like to be recognized.) Remember, you may be the only person in your Team Member's life (or Practice Member's life, for that matter) that truly recognizes them. This is an essential nutrient for human beings. Creating the environment that provides this nutrient will energize your Team and your practice.

**Celebration** is more team oriented. It's about celebrating when you hit goals and milestones. It's important to celebrate as a team when you win. Chiropractors typically suck at this because we're usually so On-Purpose and driven—with our eyes on the prize—that we run through our goals without stopping to celebrate together and appreciate the others who made it possible. It's important for all of us to remember to celebrate, to breathe in the joy of our achievements as we go. Celebration is an easy (and fun!) way to energize your practice...

And remember: **Your Practice is a Reflection of Your Energy.**

For a free training on this, check out the e=mc2 training module from the TRP Academy: *theremarkablepractice.com/Energy*.

## WHAT'S IMPORTANT NOW (WIN)

Generating energy in your practice is step one. Now your job as Chief Energy Officer is to determine *where to point that energy*.

Think of your Team's energy as sunbeams. When these beams spread out all over, they warm a surface, but not much happens. When you gather these beams together—like collecting them with a magnifying glass—wherever you point that beam, you'll start a fire.

**This is where *energy* meets *focus*.**

Start with the question, "What's important now?" (W.I.N.) Look, there are lots of moving parts in any practice. Lots of busyness. Your job as leader is to create focus, and to get people to focus their energy on something specific, a specific behavior or outcome.

**There's always going to be a lot going on, but what's important now?**

As the CEO, you must think of yourself as that lens gathering up everybody's sunrays. All their energy comes together and creates a concentrated beam toward some specific focal point. Now it's up to you. Where do you want to point that lens?

Where do you want that fire—that spark—to happen?

This is the "W.I.N." methodology. What's Important Now? (represented by the acronym W.I.N.) made famous by legendary college football coach, Lou Holtz. Coach Holtz used to remind his players at Notre Dame to ask themselves this important question throughout the day. If you want to WIN, you should do the same. Create a culture where your Team is asking themselves this question—during Pre-Shift Huddle, regular Adjustment Prime Time flow, New Patient Processing, Special Appointments and Report Time (regardless of their role on the team).

**What's Important Now?**

This codifying question will create greater clarity and focus for you and your Team. And remember: focus makes the difference between busyness and productivity.

## SUMMARY

- Your practice (business) is a reflection of your energy—your energy as the leader, your Team's energy and your patients'/Practice Members/customers' energy.
- Energy up, practice is up. Energy flat, practice is flat. Energy down, practice is down.
- You are the CEO: Chief Energy Officer. It's your responsibility to monitor, influence, and direct your Team's energy.
- This must be systematized.
- The Energy Equation is $E = mc^2$ (Energy = Money X Crucial Communications)
- There are five *Crucial Communications*:
  - Vision Casting: People want to know what success looks like.
  - Expectations and Agreements: People need clarity on what's expected of them.
  - Training and Equipping: People want to be excellent at what they do.
  - Guardrails and Discipline: People respond well to boundaries and guidelines.

- ○ Recognition and Celebration: People flourish in environments that feed their soul.
- Magnifying Lens: The CEO's job is to gather everyone's energy and direct it.
- Create clarity for the Team: this is What's Important Now and this is What's Important Next (W.I.N./W.I.N.)

*To Download All the Chapter Resources, Go Here:*
1. theremarkablepractice.com/Energy

*To Learn More, Check Out These Remarkable Resources*
2. TRP Academy: theremarkablepractice.com/tbr-academy
3. TRP DC and CA Process and Procedure Manuals: theremarkablepractice.com/tbr-manuals
4. Remarkable Private Coaching: theremarkablepractice.com/tbr-coaching
5. Remarkable Live Immersion Events: theremarkablepractice.com/tbr-events

1          2          3          4          5

CONCLUSION

# NOW MAKE IT HAPPEN

*"Good ideas are great, but implementation is everything."*
—Peter Drucker

Ultimately, what I've laid out through this book is a **Success Map**. It's a blueprint for how to do this *right*. How to take your job and turn it into a real *business*—one that is Scalable, Durable, and Transferable. And how to solve the three-dimensional Puzzle of Practice Success through each side of the Rubik's Cube: Vision, Leadership, Systems, Team, Training, and Energy.

I hope you have found this treasure map helpful. But all the best information and direction in the world is useless if you don't actually apply it. Execution is everything.

There are going to be some people who pick up the book, finger through it, take a high-level pass on it but never really dive in. Others will start the book but not finish. Or read it all the way through, then put it back on the shelf and say to themselves, "Well, that was stimulating."

But then there are the readers who will dive in and really do the work. Leverage the resources. Dig into the exercises. They are the ones who will get the results and outcomes.

> *Success is reserved for the action taker.*

The question is *not*: what did you get out of this book? The real question is: what are you going to do with it now?

It's the same with our patients. We can tell them exactly what they need to *start doing* and *stop doing* in their lives to reach their health goals. But it's up to them. The difference between those who act and those who don't is, obviously, massive. The ones who *do* what we recommend get better outcomes and have better lives. Nothing changes for the patients who do not take action.

And as with patients, what I've outlined for you through this book is not a "done for you" program; it's a "done with you" program. I wish I *could* do it all for you, but I can't. You've got to do the work.

What I can tell you is: **you can do it and it is worth it**. You can have a Remarkable Practice as *part* of a Remarkable Life. You can join the thousands of doctors who have done the work and are now reaping the rewards. The juice is worth the squeeze.

Close your eyes and imagine yourself on the other side of this process. Imagine you have implemented this transformative program. Close your eyes and see *your* Remarkable Team executing the Remarkable Process. Picture your office filled with Ideal Patients—"Understanders" who want Chiropractic because they understand Chiropractic. See *your* practice "flow" with ease and efficiency. Feel the energy and fulfillment of doing your best work—for the greatest number of people—making a bigger impact and a bigger income.

How would this change your life? Your family's life? Your Team's? Your patients'?

> *This book could literally be an inflection point for your whole career and life.*

What you've read is the culmination of everything I've learned over the last twenty-five-plus years studying Practice Success. I've curated this information through countless hours of study and reading and seminars and coaches and mentorships. I've spent hundreds of thousands of dollars on discovery and development and a million more on trial and error. You are holding the result in your hands: **The Remarkable Practice System**.

The value of what we have laid out for you in this book—and in all the additional resources available online in **The Remarkable Practice Academy**—cannot be overstated. But now, again, the question is: what are you going to do with all of it?

## WHAT THE WORLD NEEDS NOW

As I have evolved in my career from a practitioner and clinician to coach, my Purpose has shifted as well—from helping patients embrace chiropractic as a lifestyle success strategy to helping other chiropractors do a better job of serving their Purpose.

Here is my premise:

> *What the world needs now is Chiropractic, and what Chiropractic needs now is more successful chiropractors.*

What do I mean by *successful*? As I've said—that is up to you. How you define success is what's important. When you have achieved *alignment* between your **Core Values**, your **Vision Story** and your **Behaviors**—that is where success lives. That is where you will find energy, passion, fulfillment, and harmony. And the excitement, health and happiness that you experience there is the most attractive force on the planet.

If we can all agree that the goal is to have a Remarkable Practice as Part of a **Remarkable Life**, then you will have to define those things for yourself. What does a Remarkable Life mean for you? What does a **Remarkable Practice** mean for you? Remember, *clarity* is the greatest accelerant.

Patients will seek you out for many reasons. But what they discover when they find you is often so much more. They are typically looking for a solution to a problem that they think they understand—what they find is *a better way.*

How exciting it is that we get to show people a better way to better health. How fulfilling it is to see people change their thinking and then their behaviors. How satisfying to see people get their health back—get their hope back—and then take responsibility for their health outcomes.

The work that you do is truly Remarkable. It is notable; worthy of comment. It should be the talk of the town.

Chiropractic is Remarkable. Your practice is Remarkable. Your Team is Remarkable.

You are Remarkable. Now go make a difference.

# NEXT STEPS

1. Have your entire Leadership Team read this book.

2. Host the Board Meetings for your Team.

3. Establish a Meeting Rhythm for your organization:
   a. Quarterly Board Meetings
   b. Monthly Meet-Ups
   c. Weekly Team Meetings and Trainings
   d. Daily Huddles

4. Establish a metric tracking system (i.e., Vital Signs).

5. Create your Organizational Chart and your Accountability Chart.

6. Complete the Goal Setting Form.

7. Establish Training Culture
   a. Define Systems for Attraction, Conversion, Retention and Team Building
   b. Capture in written Operations Manuals—keep current
   c. Leverage video training resources (i.e., The Remarkable Practice Academy)
   d. Establish Training Curriculum
   e. Set Training Schedule and execute weekly
   f. Attend live training events with your Team (see: TRP Live Events)
   g. Leverage Coaching to help you gain clarity and hold you accountable

8. Download the resources available to you from each chapter in the book.

# AD PAGES

*TRP Academy Ad*

*TRP Manuals Ad*

*TRP Remarkable CEO Program Ad*

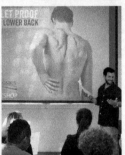

*TRP Body
Signals Ad*

# APPENDIX

Included are the reference materials for the four domains of practice success: Attraction, Conversion, Retention and Team Building. All of these resources and the associated videos that unpack each resource are available to you as part of training in the Remarkable Practice Academy.

# ATTRACTION

# BODY SIGNALS MARKETING CALENDAR

*Body Signals
Marketing
Calendar*

| JANUARY | FEBRUARY | MARCH |
|---|---|---|
| Body Signals Topic:<br>**ENERGY** | Body Signals Topic:<br>**IMMUNE SYSTEM** | Body Signals Topic:<br>**LOW BACK** |
| Workshop Title:<br>**HOW TO RECOVER<br>AFTER THE HOLIDAYS** | Workshop Title:<br>**BOOST YOUR IMMUNE<br>SYSTEM IN 21 DAYS** | Workshop Title:<br>**BULLET PROOF YOUR<br>LOW BACK** |
| APRIL | MAY | JUNE |
| Body Signals Topic:<br>**BREATHING ISSUES** | Body Signals Topic:<br>**WEIGHT LOSS** | Body Signals Topic:<br>**UPPER EXTREMITY** |
| Workshop Title:<br>**END ALLERGIES AND<br>ASTHMA** | Workshop Title:<br>**GET 15 POUNDS HEALTHIER<br>IN 15 WEEKS** | Workshop Title:<br>**F.A.S. "FALLING APART<br>SYNDROME" (PART 1)** |
| JULY | AUGUST | SEPTEMBER |
| Body Signals Topic:<br>**LOWER EXTREMITY** | Body Signals Topic:<br>**NECK PAIN** | Body Signals Topic:<br>**HEADACHES** |
| Workshop Title:<br>**F.A.S. "FALLING APART<br>SYNDROME" (PART 2)** | Workshop Title:<br>**STOP NECK PAIN FOREVER** | Workshop Title:<br>**END HEADACHES NOW** |
| OCTOBER | NOVEMBER | DECEMBER |
| Body Signals Topic:<br>**SLEEP PROBLEMS** | Body Signals Topic:<br>**DIGESTIVE ISSUES** | Body Signals Topic:<br>**STRESS** |
| Workshop Title:<br>**SLEEP BETTER TONIGHT!** | Workshop Title:<br>**ELIMINATE DIGESTIVE<br>ISSUES** | Workshop Title:<br>**STRESSED OUT?<br>THE HOLIDAY RED ZONE** |

# BODY SIGNALS IMPLEMENTATION CHECKLIST

**Good ideas are great, but implementation is everything**

| ✓ | Week 1: Do This for Current Month | Initial | ✓ | Prep This for Next Month | Initial |
|---|---|---|---|---|---|
| | Change Facebook Cover Image on Practice FB Page | | | Order Postcards, Referral Cards, from Printer for next month | |
| | Set up FB Event Description / Image on Practice FB page | | | Print out RTM Handouts for next month (or order from printer) | |
| | Set up RTM Week 1 TV Episode | | | Print out Workshop Flyer for the next month (or order from printer) | |
| | Set up RTM In-Office Video for the Month | | | | |
| | Start Email Campaign | | | | |
| | Post Workshop Promo Videos on Blog / Social Media (FB, Instagram, etc) | | | | |
| | Post Blog Post & RTM Videos for Week 1 | | | | |
| | Handout Workshop Promotional Flyers, Referral Cards, RTM Articles | | | | |
| | Review RTM Doctor's Brief (Dr) | | | | |
| | Watch Dr Jeff's RTM FB Live Training (Dr) | | | | |

| ✓ | Week 2: Do This for Current Month | Initial | ✓ | Prep This for Next Month | Initial |
|---|---|---|---|---|---|
| | Continue Email Campaign | | | Set up Next Month's Email Campaign - link to Workshop Promo videos | |
| | Post Blog Post & RTM Videos for Week 2 | | | | |
| | Set up RTM Week 2 TV Episode | | | | |
| | Dr to jump on FB Live Training for Step-by-Step Workshop Slide / Script review | | | | |
| | Dr to Finalize his Workshop Script | | | | |

| ✓ | Week 3: Do This for Current Month | Initial | ✓ | Prep This for Next Month | Initial |
|---|---|---|---|---|---|
| | Post Blog Post & RTM Videos for Week 3 | | | Mail out Postcards for next month's Workshop | |
| | Set up RTM Week 3 TV Episode | | | | |
| | Continue Email Campaign | | | | |
| | Dr to watch Dr Bobby Ilijasevic's Live Workshop Presentation on FB Live | | | | |

| ✓ | Week 4: Do This for Current Month | Initial | ✓ | Prep This for Next Month | Initial |
|---|---|---|---|---|---|
| | Print out Workshop Attendee PPT Notes Handout for upcoming workshop | | | | |
| | Set up RTM Week 4 TV Episode | | | | |
| | Dr to jump on FB Live Social Q&A call for any last minute questions | | | | |
| | HOLD WORKSHOP | | | | |

*Body Signals Implementation Checklist*

# NEW BUSINESS DEVELOPMENT REPORT

the
**REMARKABLE**
practice

*New Business Development Report*

| _____ 20 _____ | Promotional Activity | | Leads | | New Patients | | Conversions | |
|---|---|---|---|---|---|---|---|---|
| | | | G | O | G | O | G | O |
| Week 1 | Internal: | Internal: | | | | | | |
| | External: | External: | | | | | | |
| | Digital: | Digital: | | | | | | |
| Week 2 | Internal: | Internal: | | | | | | |
| | External: | External: | | | | | | |
| | Digital: | Digital: | | | | | | |
| Week 3 | Internal: | Internal: | | | | | | |
| | External: | External: | | | | | | |
| | Digital: | Digital: | | | | | | |
| Week 4 | Internal: | Internal: | | | | | | |
| | External: | External: | | | | | | |
| | Digital: | Digital: | | | | | | |
| Week 5 | Internal: | Internal: | | | | | | |
| | External: | External: | | | | | | |
| | Digital: | Digital: | | | | | | |

G = Goal

O = Outcome

| TOTALS | Leads | | New Patients | | Conversions | |
|---|---|---|---|---|---|---|
| | G | O | G | O | G | O |
| **Internal Total** | 0 | 0 | 0 | 0 | 0 | 0 |
| **External Total** | 0 | 0 | 0 | 0 | 0 | 0 |
| **Digital Total** | 0 | 0 | 0 | 0 | 0 | 0 |
| **Aggregate Total** | 0 | 0 | 0 | 0 | 0 | 0 |

# GOAL SETTING

Quarter: ( ) _____

*Goal Setting*

| Domain | KPI | Benchmark | Goal | Activity | Outcome |
|---|---|---|---|---|---|
| **Attraction** | 1. | | | | |
| | 2. | | | | |
| | 3. | | | | |

| Domain | KPI | Benchmark | Goal | Activity | Outcome |
|---|---|---|---|---|---|
| **Conversion** | 1. | | | | |
| | 2. | | | | |
| | 3. | | | | |

| Domain | KPI | Benchmark | Goal | Activity | Outcome |
|---|---|---|---|---|---|
| **Retention** | 1. | | | | |
| | 2. | | | | |
| | 3. | | | | |

| Domain | KPI | Benchmark | Goal | Activity | Outcome |
|---|---|---|---|---|---|
| **Collections** | 1. | | | | |
| | 2. | | | | |
| | 3. | | | | |

# HUDDLE SHEET

| Day: | Date:____/____/_____ | Week: ( ___ of ___ ) |
|---|---|---|

| Marketing Theme: | | |
|---|---|---|

| Marketing Event: | Goal: |
|---|---|
| | Guests: |
| | Leads: |

*Huddle Sheet*

| Patient of the Week: | Chiro Kid of the Month: |
|---|---|
| Success Story: | Practice of the Week (Topic): |

| Today | Scheduled | Capacity | Goal | Outcome | (+/−) |
|---|---|---|---|---|---|
| Patient Visits | | | | | |
| Kept Visit % | N/A | N/A | | | |
| New Patients | | | | | |
| Day 2s | | | | | |
| Progress Exams | | | | | |
| Re-Exams | | | | | |
| Re-Reports | | | | | |
| Services | | N/A | | | |
| Collections | | N/A | | | |

- ◉ Reading
- ◉ Affirmation
- ◉ Prayer
- ◉ Music

# MARKETING RETURN ON INVESTMENT REPORT

the REMARKABLE practice

Month: _____

| Event | Time (0 - 3) | Energy (0 - 3) | Focus (0 - 3) | Money (0 - 3) | NP Leads (Scheduled) | NP Prospects (Exams) | NP Conversions | Grade (A - F) |
|-------|--------------|----------------|---------------|---------------|----------------------|----------------------|----------------|---------------|
|       |              |                |               |               |                      |                      |                |               |
|       |              |                |               |               |                      |                      |                |               |
|       |              |                |               |               |                      |                      |                |               |
|       |              |                |               |               |                      |                      |                |               |
|       |              |                |               |               |                      |                      |                |               |
|       |              |                |               |               |                      |                      |                |               |

*Marketing ROI Report*

## First Four Months: Initial Intensive Care - Flow

*First Four Months*

| | |
|---|---|
| **First 4** | |
| Day 0 | Promotional Activities: Screenings, Talks, Phone Calls |
| Day 1 | New Patient Consultation/Examination |
| Day 2 | Report of Findings/Recommendations for Care/1st Adjustment |
| Day 3 | Break-In/2nd Adjustment |
| Day 4 | 1st Regular Adjustment (in the flow) |
| Visit 5-11 | Adjustments (3 X week) |
| Visit 12 | Adjustment, 1st Progress Exam, and 1st Questionnaire |
| Visit 13 | Adjustment and 1st Progress Report<br>DC call CA with frequency and consultation recommendation (thoracic, cervical, lumbar) |
| Visit 14 | Adjustment and 1st Consultation |
| Visit 15-23 | Adjustment (2 X week – per DC recommendation) (Consultation follow-up) |
| Visit 24 | Adjustment and 2nd Progress Exam and 2nd Questionnaire |
| Visit 25 | Adjustment and 2nd Progress Report |
| Visit 26 | Adjustment and 2nd Consultation |
| Visit 27-35 | Adjustment (2 X week) |
| Visit 36 | Adjustment and Re-examination: R4 Exam and 3rd Questionnaire |
| Visit 40 | Report with New Recommendations and New Financials: R4/R5 |

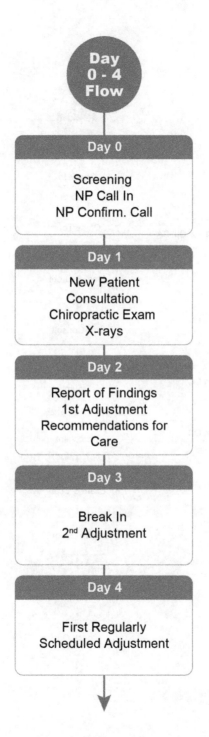

*First Four Days*

**Day 0 - 4 Flow**

**Day 0**

Screening
NP Call In
NP Confirm. Call

**Day 1**

New Patient
Consultation
Chiropractic Exam
X-rays

**Day 2**

Report of Findings
1st Adjustment
Recommendations for
Care

**Day 3**

Break In
2nd Adjustment

**Day 4**

First Regularly
Scheduled Adjustment

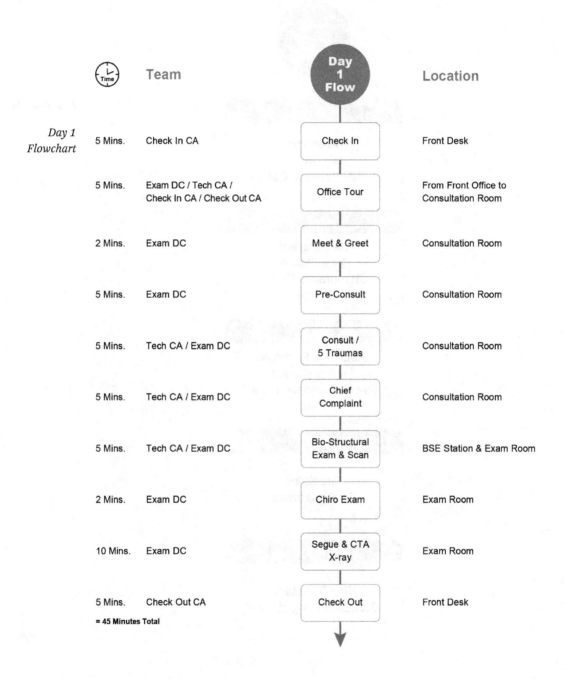

| Time | Team | Day 1 Flow | Location |
|------|------|------------|----------|
| 5 Mins. | Check In CA | Check In | Front Desk |
| 5 Mins. | Exam DC / Tech CA / Check In CA / Check Out CA | Office Tour | From Front Office to Consultation Room |
| 2 Mins. | Exam DC | Meet & Greet | Consultation Room |
| 5 Mins. | Exam DC | Pre-Consult | Consultation Room |
| 5 Mins. | Tech CA / Exam DC | Consult / 5 Traumas | Consultation Room |
| 5 Mins. | Tech CA / Exam DC | Chief Complaint | Consultation Room |
| 5 Mins. | Tech CA / Exam DC | Bio-Structural Exam & Scan | BSE Station & Exam Room |
| 2 Mins. | Exam DC | Chiro Exam | Exam Room |
| 10 Mins. | Exam DC | Segue & CTA X-ray | Exam Room |
| 5 Mins. | Check Out CA | Check Out | Front Desk |

*Day 1 Flowchart*

= 45 Minutes Total

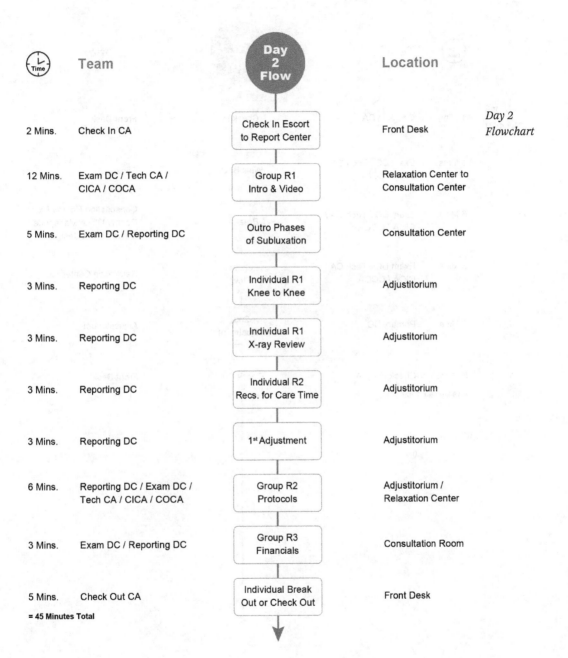

| Time | Team | Day 2 Flow | Location |
|---|---|---|---|
| 2 Mins. | Check In CA | Check In Escort to Report Center | Front Desk |
| 12 Mins. | Exam DC / Tech CA / CICA / COCA | Group R1 Intro & Video | Relaxation Center to Consultation Center |
| 5 Mins. | Exam DC / Reporting DC | Outro Phases of Subluxation | Consultation Center |
| 3 Mins. | Reporting DC | Individual R1 Knee to Knee | Adjustitorium |
| 3 Mins. | Reporting DC | Individual R1 X-ray Review | Adjustitorium |
| 3 Mins. | Reporting DC | Individual R2 Recs. for Care Time | Adjustitorium |
| 3 Mins. | Reporting DC | 1st Adjustment | Adjustitorium |
| 6 Mins. | Reporting DC / Exam DC / Tech CA / CICA / COCA | Group R2 Protocols | Adjustitorium / Relaxation Center |
| 3 Mins. | Exam DC / Reporting DC | Group R3 Financials | Consultation Room |
| 5 Mins. | Check Out CA | Individual Break Out or Check Out | Front Desk |

**= 45 Minutes Total**

*Day 2 Flowchart*

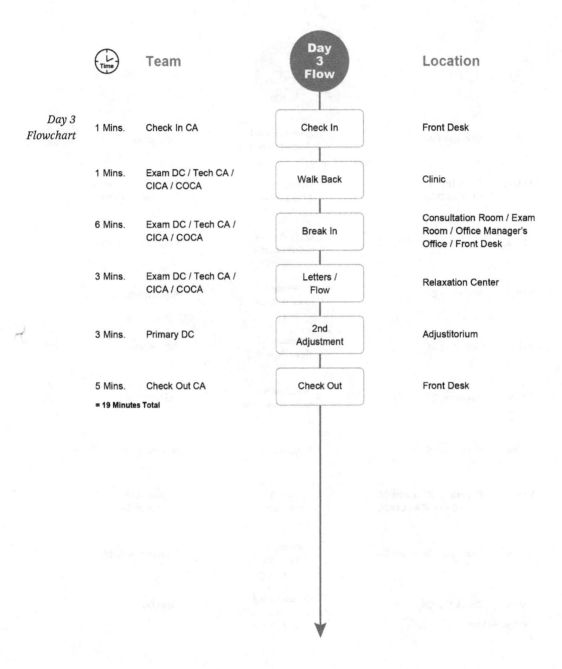

**Time**

**Team**

**Day 3 Flow**

**Location**

| Time | Team | Flow | Location |
|---|---|---|---|
| 1 Mins. | Check In CA | Check In | Front Desk |
| 1 Mins. | Exam DC / Tech CA / CICA / COCA | Walk Back | Clinic |
| 6 Mins. | Exam DC / Tech CA / CICA / COCA | Break In | Consultation Room / Exam Room / Office Manager's Office / Front Desk |
| 3 Mins. | Exam DC / Tech CA / CICA / COCA | Letters / Flow | Relaxation Center |
| 3 Mins. | Primary DC | 2nd Adjustment | Adjustitorium |
| 5 Mins. | Check Out CA | Check Out | Front Desk |

**= 19 Minutes Total**

# OFFICE POLICIES: "BREAK-IN" FORM

| Expectations and Agreements | | |
|---|---|---|
| ☐ **Care Plan** | ⦿ Time Period<br>⦿ Visit Frequency | ⦿ Progress Exams / Reports<br>⦿ Re-Exams / Reports |
| ☐ **Scheduling** | ⦿ Mapped Out<br>⦿ Compliance | ⦿ Rescheduling<br>⦿ 3 Strike Rule |
| ☐ **Workshop**<br>**Better Results**<br>**Faster (BRF)** | ⦿ Scheduled<br>⦿ Rule of 72 | ⦿ Recording / Questionnaire<br>⦿ Guests (Spouse, Family, Friends) |
| ☐ **Family**<br>**Check-Up** | ⦿ Spouse<br>⦿ Children | ⦿ Referral Coupons<br>⦿ |
| ☐ **Other**<br>_____ | ⦿<br>⦿ | ⦿<br>⦿ |

| New Patient Conversion Performance Report | | | | | | | |
|---|---|---|---|---|---|---|---|
| **Week** | **Leads** | **Day 1** | **Day 2** | **Day 3** | **Day 4** | **Conv. #** | **Conv. %** |
| 1 | | | | | | | |
| 2 | | | | | | | |
| 3 | | | | | | | |
| 4 | | | | | | | |
| 5 | | | | | | | |
| Totals | | | | | | | |

# TRP TROUBLESHOOTING FORM

*Troubleshooting Form*

| Domain | Team Member (Name) | Issue |
|---|---|---|
| **Attraction** | | |
| ◉    Internal Marketing | | |
| ◉    Digital Marketing | | |
| ◉    External Marketing | | |
| **Conversion** | | |
| **Retention** | | |
| **Team Building (Training)** | | |
| ◉    DCs | | |
| ◉    CAs | | |
| **Collections** | | |
| **Issue / Problem** | | |
| 1.    Vision | | |
| 2.    Leadership | | |
| 3.    Systems | | |
| 4.    People | | |
| 5.    Training | | |
| 6.    Energy | | |

# CONVERSION

# "THE PATH" WORKSHEET:
# RECOMMENDATIONS FOR CARE

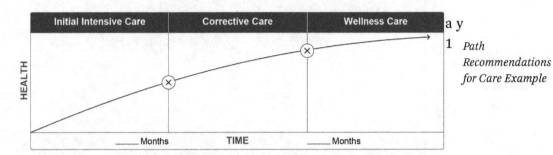

a y

1 *Path Recommendations for Care Example*

| Mo | Exam | | Stage | | Frequency Time @ Visits |
|----|------|--|-------|--|-------------------------|
|    |      |  |       |  | @ |
|    |      |  |       |  | @ |
|    |      |  |       |  | @ |
|    |      |  |       |  | @ |
|    |      |  |       |  | @ |
|    |      |  |       |  | @ |

EXAMPLE:

| Mo | Exam | | Stage | | Frequency Time @ Visits |
|----|------|--|-------|--|-------------------------|
| 0 | NP Exam | NP | Initial Intensive Care | IC | 4 Weeks @ 3 x Week |
| 1 | Progress Exam 1 | PE1 | Initial Intensive Care | IC | 6 Weeks @ 2 x Week |
| 2 | Progress Exam 2 | PE2 | Initial Intensive Care | IC | 6 Weeks @ 2 x Week |
| 4 | Re-Exam 1 | R4 | Corrective Care | CC | 52 Weeks @ 1 x Week |
| 16 | Re-Exam 2 | R5 | Wellness / Maintenance | WC | 52 Weeks @ 1 x Week |
| 28 | Wellness Review | R6 | Wellness / Maintenance | WC | 52 Weeks @ 1 x Week |

# "THE PATH" WORKSHEET: RECOMMENDATIONS FOR CARE

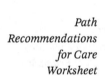

*Path Recommendations for Care Worksheet*

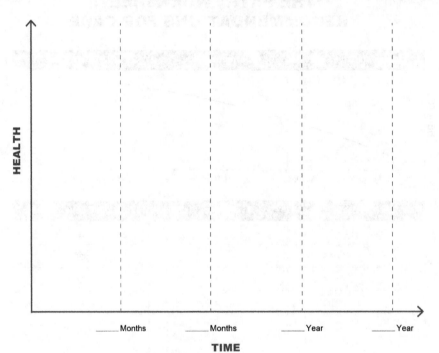

# "THE PLAN": FINANCIAL PLAN WORKSHEET

| Service | # | Charge Per | Total | |
|---|---|---|---|---|
| ADJUSTMENT | | $ | $ | |
| PE | | $ | $ | |
| RE | | $ | $ | |
| CONSULTS | | $ | $ | |
| OTHER: | | $ | $ | |
| OTHER: | | $ | $ | |
| OTHER: | | $ | $ | |
| | | | Total $: Retail Value: | |
| OPTION 1 | _____ Equal payments of $ _____ | | Total Plan Fee: $ | Save: % $ |
| OPTION 2 | $_____ Down + ___ Equal pays of $_____ | | Total Plan Fee: $ | Save: % $ |
| INSURANCE | Notes: | | | |
| OTHER: | *Example:* Multiple Family Member Discount | | Less (%): | Save: % $ |

*Financial Plan Worksheet*

*Strategic*
*Schedule*

| 🕐 | Monday | Tuesday | Wednesday | Thursday | Friday | Saturday |
|---|---|---|---|---|---|---|
| 6:45 | Pre-Shift Huddle | Pre-Shift Huddle | | Pre-Shift Huddle | | |
| 7:00 | | | | | | |
| 7:15 | | | | | | |
| 7:30 | | | | | | |
| 7:45 | Adjusting & New Patients Day 1 | Adjusting & New Patients Day 1 | | Adjusting & New Patients Day 1 | | |
| 8:00 | | | | | | |
| 8:15 | | | | | | |
| 8:30 | | | | | | |
| 8:45 | | | | | | |
| 9:00 | | | | | | |
| 9:15 | | | | | | |
| 9:30 | | | | | | |
| 9:45 | Report Time Day 2 (R1/2/3) | Report Time Re-commitment (R4/5) | | Report Time Day 2 (R1/2/3) | | |
| 10:00 | | | | | | |
| 10:15 | | | | | | |
| 10:30 | | | OFFICE CLOSED | | | |
| 10:45 | | | | | | |
| 11:00 | | | | | | |
| 11:15 | Adjusting & New Patients Day 1 | Adjusting & New Patients Day 1 | | Adjusting & New Patients Day 1 | | |
| 11:30 | | | | | | |
| 11:45 | | | | | | |
| 12:00 | | | | | | |
| 12:15 | Post Shift Huddle | Post Shift Huddle | | Post Shift Huddle | | |
| 12:30 | | | | | OFFICE CLOSED | OFFICE CLOSED |
| 12:45 | | BRF Workshop Alternating Weeks* | | | | |
| 13:00 | | | | | | |
| 13:15 | OFFICE CLOSED | | | OFFICE CLOSED | | |
| 13:30 | | | | | | |
| 13:45 | | | | | | |
| 14:00 | | | | | | |
| 14:15 | | | | | | |
| 14:30 | | | | | | |
| 14:45 | Pre-Shift Huddle | | Pre-Shift Huddle | Pre-Shift Huddle | | |
| 15:00 | | | | | | |
| 15:15 | Adjusting & New Patients Day 1 | | Adjusting & New Patients Day 1 | Adjusting & New Patients Day 1 | | |
| 15:30 | | | | | | |
| 15:45 | | | | | | |
| 16:00 | | OFFICE CLOSED | | | | |
| 16:15 | | | | | | |
| 16:30 | | | | | | |
| 16:45 | Report Time Day 2 (R1/2/3) | | Report Time Day 2 (R1/2/3) | Report Time Re-Commitment (R4/5) | | |
| 17:00 | | | | | | |
| 17:15 | | | | | | |
| 17:30 | Adjusting & New Patients Day 1 | | Adjusting & New Patients Day 1 | Adjusting & New Patients Day 1 | | |
| 17:45 | | | | | | |
| 18:00 | | | | | | |
| 18:15 | Post Shift Huddle | | Post Shift Huddle | Post Shift Huddle | | |
| 18:30 | | | | | | |
| 18:45 | | | BRF Workshop Alternating Weeks* | | | |
| 19:00 | | | | | | |
| 19:15 | | | | | | |

| ⏰ | Monday | Tuesday | Wednesday | Thursday | Friday | Saturday |
|---|--------|---------|-----------|----------|--------|----------|
| 6:45 | Pre-Shift Huddle | Pre-Shift Huddle | | Pre-Shift Huddle | | |
| 7:00 | | | | | | |
| 7:15 | | | | | | |
| 7:30 | | | OFFICE CLOSED | | OFFICE CLOSED | OFFICE CLOSED |
| 7:45 | Adjusting & New Patients Day 1 | Adjusting & New Patients Day 1 | | Adjusting & New Patients Day 1 | | |
| 8:00 | | | | | | |
| 8:15 | | | | | | |
| 8:30 | | | | | | |
| 8:45 | | | | | | |
| 9:00 | | | | | | |
| 9:15 | | | | | | |
| 9:30 | | | | | | |
| 9:45 | Report Time Day 2 (R1/2/3) | Report Time Re-Commitment (R4/5) | | Report Time Day 2 (R1/2/3) | | |
| 10:00 | | | | | | |
| 10:15 | | | | | | |
| 10:30 | | | | | | |
| 10:45 | | | Marketing Shift | | Marketing Shift | Marketing Shift |
| 11:00 | | | | | | |
| 11:15 | Adjusting & New Patients Day 1 | | | Adjusting & New Patients Day 1 | | |
| 11:30 | | | | | | |
| 11:45 | | | | | | |
| 12:00 | | | | | | |
| 12:15 | Post Shift Huddle | Post Shift Huddle | | Post Shift Huddle | | |
| 12:30 | | | | | | |
| 12:45 | OFFICE CLOSED | BRF Workshop Alternating Weeks* | | OFFICE CLOSED | | |
| 13:00 | | | OFFICE CLOSED | | | |
| 13:15 | | | | | | |
| 13:30 | | | | | | |
| 13:45 | | | | | | |
| 14:00 | Team Meeting | Team Training | Team Training | Marketing Meeting | | |
| 14:15 | | | | | | |
| 14:30 | | | | | | |
| 14:45 | Pre-Shift Huddle | | Pre-Shift Huddle | Pre-Shift Huddle | | |
| 15:00 | | | | | | |
| 15:15 | Adjusting & New Patients Day 1 | | Adjusting & New Patients Day 1 | Adjusting & New Patients Day 1 | OFFICE CLOSED | OFFICE CLOSED |
| 15:30 | | | | | | |
| 15:45 | | | | | | |
| 16:00 | | | | | | |
| 16:15 | | Marketing Shift | | | | |
| 16:30 | | | | | | |
| 16:45 | Report Time Day 2 (R1/2/3) | | Report Time Day 2 (R1/2/3) | Report Time Re-Commitment (R4/5) | | |
| 17:00 | | | | | | |
| 17:15 | | | | | | |
| 17:30 | Adjusting & New Patients Day 1 | | Adjusting & New Patients Day 1 | Adjusting & New Patients Day 1 | | |
| 17:45 | | | | | | |
| 18:00 | | | | | | |
| 18:15 | Post Shift Huddle | | Post Shift Huddle | Post Shift Huddle | | |
| 18:30 | | | | | | |
| 18:45 | | | BRF Workshop Alternating Weeks* | | | |
| 19:00 | | | | | | |
| 19:15 | | | | | | |

*Strategic Schedule with Team*

# RETENTION

## GOAL SETTING

*Goal Setting*

Quarter: ( ) _____

| Domain | KPI | Benchmark | Goal | Activity | Outcome |
|--------|-----|-----------|------|----------|---------|
| Attraction | 1. | | | | |
| | 2. | | | | |
| | 3. | | | | |
| Domain | KPI | Benchmark | Goal | Activity | Outcome |
| Conversion | 1. | | | | |
| | 2. | | | | |
| | 3. | | | | |
| Domain | KPI | Benchmark | Goal | Activity | Outcome |
| Retention | 1. | | | | |
| | 2. | | | | |
| | 3. | | | | |
| Domain | KPI | Benchmark | Goal | Activity | Outcome |
| Collections | 1. | | | | |
| | 2. | | | | |
| | 3. | | | | |

# HUDDLE SHEET

*Huddle Sheet*

| Day: | Date:___/___/_____ | | Week: ( ___ of ___ ) |
|---|---|---|---|
| Marketing Theme: | | | |

| Marketing Event: | | Goal: |
|---|---|---|
| | | Guests: |
| | | Leads: |

| Patient of the Week: | Chiro Kid of the Month: |
|---|---|
| Success Story: | Practice of the Week (Topic): |

| Today | Scheduled | Capacity | Goal | Outcome | ( +⁄- ) |
|---|---|---|---|---|---|
| Patient Visits | | | | | |
| Kept Visit % | N/A | N/A | | | |
| New Patients | | | | | |
| Day 2s | | | | | |
| Progress Exams | | | | | |
| Re-Exams | | | | | |
| Re-Reports | | | | | |
| Services | | N/A | | | |
| Collections | | N/A | | | |

- ◉ Reading
- ◉ Affirmation
- ◉ Prayer
- ◉ Music

# REMARKABLE TEAM MEETINGS

*Remarkable
Team Meetings*

| Name: | Date:___/___/_____ |
|---|---|

| KPI | Activity / Focus | Comments: Wins / Challenges |
|---|---|---|
| 1. | Last Week: | |
| | This Week: | |
| | Next Week: | |
| 2. | Last Week: | |
| | This Week: | |
| | Next Week: | |
| 3. | Last Week: | |
| | This Week: | |
| | Next Week: | |
| 4. | Last Week: | |
| | This Week: | |
| | Next Week: | |
| 5. | Last Week: | |
| | This Week: | |
| | Next Week: | |

| Take-Aways | Action Items | Notes |
|---|---|---|
| | | |
| | | |
| | | |
| | | |

# TRP SCORECARD: INDIVIDUAL

the REMARKABLE practice

*Scorecard—*
*Individual*

| Team Member: | Primary Objectives |
|---|---|
| Position: | 1. |
| Date:____/____/____ | 2. |
| Quarter: (  )_____ | 3. |

**Top 5 Priorities**

| | KPI | Key Performance Indicator | Benchmark | Goal | Result | Action Item |
|---|---|---|---|---|---|---|
| 1 | | | | | | |
| 2 | | | | | | |
| 3 | | | | | | |
| 4 | | | | | | |
| 5 | | | | | | |

**Monthly Meet-Up**       Month 1                       Month 2                       Month 3

| | KPI | Status | Notes | Status | Notes | Result | Notes |
|---|---|---|---|---|---|---|---|
| 1 | | | | | | | |
| 2 | | | | | | | |
| 3 | | | | | | | |
| 4 | | | | | | | |
| 5 | | | | | | | |

Status:    (+) = Ahead     (Δ) = On Track     (-) = Behind

# TRP TROUBLESHOOTING FORM

*Troubleshooting Form*

| Domain | Team Member (Name) | Issue |
|---|---|---|
| **Attraction** | | |
| ⦿ Internal Marketing | | |
| ⦿ Digital Marketing | | |
| ⦿ External Marketing | | |
| **Conversion** | | |
| **Retention** | | |
| **Team Building (Training)** | | |
| ⦿ DCs | | |
| ⦿ CAs | | |
| **Collections** | | |
| **Issue / Problem** | | |
| 1. Vision | | |
| 2. Leadership | | |
| 3. Systems | | |
| 4. People | | |
| 5. Training | | |
| 6. Energy | | |

**TEAM BUILDING**

# ACKNOWLEDGMENTS

This was a strangely difficult part of writing this book. I did not want to forget anyone but was told that only your mother will read this—be sure to thank her first. So, thank you, Mom. At risk of stating the obvious, none of this would have been possible without you. Big thank you to my father, as well. Dad you are world-class. You guys were the first to show me what remarkable means. Thank you to my beautiful and understanding wife, Camilla. Remarkable wife, remarkable life. Could not and would not want to do it without you. Thank you to my kiddos, Sam and Emma for understanding when Daddy was head-down and working. And thanks to my siblings, Kim and Jeff for their love, friendship and encouragement. Thank you to Scott, Paul and Pastor Bruce, my Brothers in Christ...And too many others to list and terrified to leave anyone out...but, here goes: Big thanks to Sheila Mielcarek, Nina Lambert, Christy Graham and the rest of The Remarkable Practice Team: Mary Quense, Laura Greer, Kate Rudd, Drs. Malcolm Rudd, Bobby and Jelena Ilijasevic, Pete Camiolo, Mark Mouw, Sebastian Bonnin, Adrian Couzner and Brett Racine. Thank you to Dr. Allen Miner and the Chiro Match Makers Team. Thank you to the early Chiropractic Pioneers: Drs. DD, BJ, Fred, Sig, Sid, Gonstead, et. al. Thank you to early mentors like Drs. Guy Reikeman, John Demartini, Coach CJ Mertz, Pat Gentempo and Chris Kent. And thank you to my modern-day friends and chiropractic warriors: The Remarkables, The Ultimate Achievers Club, Dr. Joe Esposito and the AlignLife Team, the Body Signals Team, PK and the Bonfire Health Team, The Lion Chasers, Garrett Gunderson, Billy D....and you—the DC in the trenches making a difference every day. Remember, you are in the business of saving lives—so when business is good, everybody wins.

In Health from Within,

Stephen Franson, DC

# ABOUT THE AUTHOR

Dr. Stephen Franson is a living, breathing billboard for the Chiropractic Wellness Lifestyle. Steeped in over twenty years of clinical practice and application of Wellness Principles, Franson's interface with a vibrant family practice afforded him a unique perspective on what works in healthcare—and what doesn't. As the CEO and Clinic Director of one of the most robust wellness practices on the planet, his time was spent in the trenches with families who were simply looking for a better way to better health.

Now Franson is a sought-after international coach, speaker, author, and teacher. As founder of The Remarkable Practice his Vision and influence extend well beyond the confines of a brick and mortar practice. He is also co-founder of Chiro Match Makers, a specialized placement service for Chiropractic and co-creator of the Bonfire Health Program, a web-based total wellness lifestyle transformation program.

When he is not traveling the world sharing The Remarkable Practice System, you can find him at his New Hampshire Seacoast home with his family pursuing their passion of winter surfing in the coldest water in the world.